A STRANGER in the WILL

by

B. L. Marshall

A Stranger in the Will

If you purchased this book without a cover you should be aware that this book is stolen property. It was reported as "unsold and destroyed" to the publisher, and neither the author nor the publisher has received any payment for this "stripped book."

All rights reserved. Except for use in any review, the reproduction or utilization of this work in whole or in part in any form by any electronic, mechanical or other means, now known or hereafter invented, including xerography, photocopying and recording, or in any information storage or retrieval system, is forbidden without the written permission of B. L. Marshall.

This is a work of fiction. Names, characters, places and incidents are either the product of the author's imagination or are used fictitiously , and any resemblance to actual persons, living or dead, business establishments, events or locales is entirely coincidental.

Copyright 2018 B. L. Marshall

All rights reserved.

ISBN-13:978-1484041475
ISBN-10:148404147X

Acknowledgements

Many people helped bring A Stranger in the Will to life. Thank you to my editor, Jasmine Hinkey, and to my daughter Tonya and her husband Shane for finding my vision in the book cover. Most of all, thank you to my husband and biggest supporter, Bruce, who spends almost as many hours preparing my books for press as I do writing them.

A Stranger in the Will

ONE

It was three o'clock in the morning when Heather woke with a pounding in her chest. She sat up and touched the lamp at her bedside. As the room became visible, she felt her fear was from a nightmare and it would soon be gone.

She had begun to calm down when she saw her husband was not in bed. Not even his impression was left on his pillow, nor was there any evidence he had ever been lying next to her.

Heather called his name, but received no response. Something made her senses whirl about in a panic as she realized the whole apartment was in darkness.

Sean had been acting strange lately, and that was cause for her to be concerned.

"Sean!" She hollered as she threw her legs over the side of the bed, stepping into her slippers and robe. Still not a sound. Going about the apartment turning on lights, Heather knew he was gone.

She tried to wait up, hoping he would come back, or at least call, but finally sleep claimed her once again as she lay on the sofa.

Waking to a noise, she thought Sean had come in. It turned out to be the faint sound of the alarm going off in the bedroom. It was 6:00 a.m., and the lights of Singapore were beginning to fade from the streets below as daylight began to take their place. She checked the bedroom when she turned off the alarm, hoping she would see Sean had come back while she slept. The bed was still empty.

Heather turned, heading toward the kitchen when she stopped, discovering that her husband's wallet and keys were still on his dresser.

Knowing now that something was very wrong, she decided it was time to call the police. After finishing with the police, she called the school to let them know she wouldn't be in. She felt guilty knowing that her students were at an important crossroads in learning the English language. She hoped skipping today's lessons would not set them back. They had come so far and fully enjoyed their classes.

TWO

The police arrived a few minutes later, Heather explained all she knew, which wasn't much. She told them Sean had been depressed for some time and began to give them a little background information.

"We moved here from Colorado almost five years ago. Sean had big plans to start a business that would set him up for life, but it didn't happen, and he couldn't get past it." She told them that she had been able to go to college and now taught third grade. They made a good living, but it wasn't enough for Sean. "I'm worried, he left without his keys and wallet. He's never done that."

The officer assured her they would check it out and let her know if they found anything. He suggested that perhaps Sean had gone for a walk and had gotten lost.

"No, I doubt that. He started drinking quite a bit, so he knew his way around town to all the bars and how to get back here when he was very drunk. I know something awful has happened, this just isn't like him."

After the police left, she stood looking out the window to the street below in hopes she would see Sean walking home.

Several hours later the phone rang. Heather quickly picked up. "Mrs. Sullivan?" a husky voice, with very good English, inquired.

"My name is Detective Olsen with the Singapore Police Department. I understand you filed a missing persons report this morning."

"Yes, I did. Have you found my husband?"

"Mrs. Sullivan, is there anyone with you who can bring you down to the station? If not, I'll come and pick you up myself."

"Detective Olsen, you didn't answer my question. Did you find him?"

"I'm sorry Mrs. Sullivan, but we have recovered a body found on the beach this morning. I need you to come down to see if it is your husband. I'll come for you if you need me to."

"No, I'll be right there." She was shaking as she hung up and wondered if it was such a good idea to go alone.

Detective Olsen walked up and introduced himself to Heather as she waited at the reception desk. "Are you sure you don't want to call someone to go in with you?"

"I don't think so, I can handle it."

"Okay, please follow me," he said as he led her down the long hallway. She suddenly felt very frightened. As they arrived at the door to enter the morgue, the detective asked her if she was ready before he opened the door. Heather took a deep breath and nodded that she was. He escorted her inside and up to the viewing window. The curtain opened from the other side. Heather opened her eyes and gasped as she focused on the only part of the body visible outside the sheet, Sean's face. She started to lose her balance. Detective Olsen caught

A Stranger in the Will

her by the elbow and held on. "Mrs. Sullivan, by your reaction I assume this is your husband, Sean Sullivan."

It was all she could do to simply nod, acknowledging his observation. He then accompanied her out of the room as he offered his sympathy.

"What happened to him?" she asked. "Did he drown?"

"Yes, he did," Olsen replied.

"Can you tell me how well he could swim? We still don't know for sure if it was accidental or if someone was with him, or if he intentionally did this to himself."

"He played football in high school, he was a quarterback. He was in very good physical shape. I know he did swim, got a couple of metals actually, but that was a long time ago. We haven't been swimming together for quite some time. I'm not sure if you lose any of the skill after awhile. As I said before, he had started drinking heavily as well."

"All right, as soon as we know anything, I'll call you. I'll get an officer to follow us in your car and I'll drive you home."

Heather just shook her head in agreement.

THREE

Later that day Detective Olsen knocked on Heather's door. When she greeted him, it was obvious she'd been crying most of the day. Her eyes were extremely puffy and there were tissues all over the coffee table. The shock of seeing him so soon registered on her face. "Come in detective. Am I correct in assuming you have information?"

"Yes, I do, can we sit down? This might take a few minutes."

"Of course, I'm sorry. Would you like some coffee?"

"No thank you. I just stopped by to tell you what the ME found." Heather sat down and waited for him to speak again. "This isn't easy to hear Mrs. Sullivan. The ME did rule your husband's death a suicide. I'm so sorry." He waited a couple of minutes to give her time to absorb the news. "I know this isn't a good time for you, but do you think you could answer a question for me?"

"Yes, if I can."

"You told the officer this morning that your husband has been depressed lately. Did you think it was bad enough to cause him to do this? I only ask as a backup to the ME's findings."

"I didn't think it was. I did ask him to talk to somebody who could help him sort it all out, but he refused. Said he'd deal with it himself. Looking at it now, I can't help but wonder if this is what he meant by...dealing with it himself'. If only I'd known he was that bad."

"Do you have any family around here that can stay with you or you with them? Or a good friend?"

"No family, but I do have friends that I can call. I was just waiting to find out what really happened."

The detective stood. "I'm so sorry for your loss Mrs. Sullivan. I hope you will be able to move on and put your own life back together soon."

Heather shook his hand and thanked him as she opened the door and said, "good-bye".

***

After a few weeks, Heather returned from taking Sean back home to Colorado for burial. She knew she had to make some changes in her life. Deciding to stay in Singapore or go back to Colorado permanently was utmost in her thoughts. If she planned to stay here, she'd have to get another apartment. She knew she couldn't stay in the one she shared with Sean. It wasn't long before she knew in her heart what she wanted. Knowing it would be hard to give up her teaching job, she chose to stay in Singapore. She had really grown to love the students she taught and didn't want to leave them.

It took only a few weeks to find the perfect place. Now standing at the window, looking at the spectacular view of this beautiful island country, she was happy with the decisions she had made. Both to stay and the new apartment she chose.

FOUR

The following summer Conrad Simms entered her life. He was a handsome, debonair man who was in Singapore on business. A love affair was born the day they met. The more time they spent together, the more she knew she was stuck, knowing full well they would never be more than secret lovers. His family in Los Angeles would always be a wedge between them. Conrad had told her about his two children and his wife.

"I have one daughter, Kylie, and a son, Jordan. Jordan is a handful and always has been. There are times I think he is the devil himself," Conrad had said. Still, Heather looked forward to each trip with more anticipation. Her life was filled with the love, the excitement and the new experiences for which she had longed for, for a very long time.

***

Time passed and suddenly her bubble burst as fast as it had appeared. A little over a year ago. She was pregnant and she started counting the days until Conrad was due back. Unfortunately, he didn't share her enthusiasm, for he left Singapore, and she never heard from him again.

Heather's life was shattered, and she soon found herself buried in her work. She was only holding it together knowing she would have a baby that would fill the emptiness that had come over her when Conrad left. But, this child growing inside her would always be a reminder of him and the love she thought they shared. Heather often wondered. *"Am I strong enough to deal with that?"*

***

However, the months past until Heather gave birth to the most beautiful baby girl. From that day on Julianne was her life. As she grew into a lovely young woman with silky black hair and enchanting green eyes, Heather had regrets that Conrad never cared to know her. It was a great loss for him. She was the kind of child anyone would be proud to call theirs.

***

Then, when Julianne was 20, Heather realized her own health was failing. She was feeling worse every day. Against her better judgment, she made a doctor's appointment, even knowing she would wish she hadn't. The testing confirmed what Heather feared, stage four cancer, too far along to treat.

It wasn't long after the diagnosis before Julianne took control, as her mother had become confined to her bed. As Heather watched her beautiful daughter, she felt more and more confident that

A Stranger in the Will

Julianne was very capable of going on alone, after she was gone.

On a sunny Saturday morning, Julianne was running a few errands as her mother napped. Heather woke to a strange noise, and there stood a tall and handsome man. She was sure her mind was playing tricks on her, it couldn't be. As her eyes focused she realized he had to be Conrad's son. He looked just like his father, but the way he hovered over her was frightening. She had no idea how she found out about her or what he wanted. As he started to speak her eyes tear up as her memories of his father took over her thoughts. She was soon brought back to the present as he made his demands very clear. He stood over her bed and explained to her, with such hatred in his eyes, that she was to discourage her daughter from ever looking for her father or anyone else involved with Conrad Simms's family. He assured her the consequences would be severe. From the look on his face she had no doubt he was dead serious. When she opened her eyes after blinking away the tears, she looked around, but Jordan Simms was gone. She was shaking from fear, but at the same time disappointed that he had gone before she could ask about Conrad.

When Julianne came in she asked her mom what was wrong. Heather simply replied that she had a bad dream.

***

Time passed quickly as Heather's condition worsened. She knew the time had come. It was imperative she get Julianne to promise she wouldn't interfere with or look for her father or his family. She never told her daughter about her visit from Jordan. Heather knew her daughter couldn't understand her strange request, but Julianne promised anyway.

***

Two days after the funeral, Julianne was left alone to go on with her life. Her mother had tried to talk her into going back to the States to be near family, but she insisted on staying in Singapore. It was the only place she'd ever known.

A Stranger in the Will

FIVE

Julianne continued to live in the apartment she and her mother had shared. She worked and went on with her life, until one day she couldn't tamp down her anger towards her father any longer. For months now she struggled to rid herself of the feeling she needed to confront him, to find out what the hell happened and why he left the woman he loved and his child, supposedly conceived in love. Why had he left her mother with a broken heart? But first she had to find out who he was. She stood looking out the very window, with the beautiful view, that had captured her mother's heart so many years ago.

***

A few weeks later, Julianne packed up her personal belongings and sold everything else. She said her good-byes and headed for the only place she knew to start, Los Angeles. She felt a pull of excitement inside herself as she boarded the flight that would change her life forever, while, at the same time, praying her mother would forgive her for breaking her promise. Finding answers to the questions she'd always be haunted by for the rest of her life, trumped that promise.

She landed at LAX exhausted and scared. She had searched on the Internet for a hotel that would be clean and safe but would not clean out her savings. Once settled in her room, she showered, had some dinner, and crashed for the night. Tomorrow her adventure for better or worse would begin.

Julianne woke the next morning, nervous but determined. She walked into the Hall of Records, not knowing where to begin. She stopped and talked to an elderly lady behind a desk. After Julianne explained her situation, the woman told her that would be difficult to eliminate so many business owners without at least a partial name. Julianne felt immediate defeat and realized she would need some help. She asked if there was a phone book she could use. The woman handed her one and pointed to a desk where she could sit down. As Julianne found the listings she was looking for, her eyes grew as big as golf balls at the number of P.I.'s listed. She started sorting by location near her hotel, then eliminated firms as she felt they would be more expensive than a one-person operation. That cut her options down considerably, yet still left too many. She walked over to the elderly woman once more, now noticing her nameplate said Mary Matthews. Julianne asked Mary if she knew of any one of the remaining investigators that would be reliable but not cost a small fortune. It just so happened that Mary's nephew was a P.I. She gave Julianne his name and phone number and told her to tell Jake that she recommended him.

SIX

Julianne thanked Mary and left. She went back to her hotel room to make her phone call. On the second ring a young women spoke. "Jake Matthews Agency, how may I help you?" Julianne wasn't sure where to begin. She explained her circumstances to the receptionist and admitted she didn't know what to do beyond making this call. Donna, the voice on the other end, told her the next move would be to make an appointment to sit down with Jake.

"Okay," Julianne said, "I would like to do that." So, the appointment was made. In two days Julianne would be sitting across a desk from a private investigator who would hopefully be able to find her father.

When Julianne entered Jake's office, she had a tingle in the pit of her stomach. She had a lot of anger built up for her father, but at the same time she felt a little bit of excitement to meet him. Jake Matthews could hopefully make that happen.

Donna took Julianne into Jake's office.

As Jake stood behind his desk, Julianne notice how strong and capable he looked. He was a nice looking man, standing behind a very messy desk, piled with stacks and stacks of papers. It made her wonder if he was too busy to take on her case.

Jake extended his hand and introduced himself. Julianne took his hand and did the same. "I want to thank you for seeing me, Mr. Matthews. Your aunt told me to be sure to tell you she recommended you. She's a very nice lady."

"Yes, she is, and she'll be expecting her commission if we strike a deal." They both laughed as Jake pointed to the chair for Julianne to sit down.

"Mr. Matthews," she began.

"Please, just call me Jake."

"Okay," Julianne blushed as she continued. "I want to find my father, but I don't even know his name." She explained the situation in detail. She told him everything she knew, which wasn't much.

"Wow," he said, "that's not much to go on." Julianne's smile faded. "I'm not saying I can't give it a try. I'm just saying it's not a lot of information to start with." He wrote down every word she said because it didn't take long.

"I'm sorry," she said. "My mother would never tell me much about him because she was afraid I would try to find him. I think she felt what little I knew would keep me from doing that."

"Do you look like your mother?"

"What?" she asked.

"If you look a lot like your mother, chances are you don't have a lot of your father's traits. But if you don't, chances are good that we could match your picture to your fathers if I get lucky and find a photo. If he owns a successful business, he's probably got a picture on the Chamber of Commerce web-site."

"My mother was blonde and blue eyed, shorter than I am." She handed him a picture.

A Stranger in the Will

"Well," Jake said as he looked from the picture to Julianne. "I guess we know who had the dominant genes, and in this case, that's a good thing. I'm going to make a copy of this picture to keep in the file in case I find him. I would also like to take a picture of you for the same reason," Jake said.

"Okay," Julianne agreed. "I guess this means you'll take my case?"

"Actually, I think it'll be very interesting. Something I haven't done too much of. Shouldn't take too long. However, I hope you realize if he never made any attempt to see you, he may not be real happy you're pursuing this." He looked at Julianne for a response.

"I know, but that's his problem. He'll have to deal with it."

They discussed the fees and came to an agreement. Jake explained how it worked and said he would start on it that afternoon and let her know what he found.

"Okay," she said. "I'll be looking forward to your call, and thank you very much."

"You're very welcome. Hopefully he's a camera hog like many rich people are in this town and we'll find out real quick who he is."

Julianne got up, shook his hand and left. Jake thought she was stunning and wondered why anyone wouldn't want her in his or her life.

SEVEN

Jake had a few appointments he needed to make on other cases but wasn't having much luck hooking up with anyone. He decided to start researching wealthy male business owners. He had an idea of the age group, he just wished he knew what kind of business he should be looking at. He found the roster for the Chamber of Commerce, hoping his subject belonged. He figured with business trips to Singapore, her father could be in sales.

He included the ideas he had into his search and came up with eight-four men. Narrowing it down to a possible age gave him sixty-seven. He typed in their names one at a time. However, no one even came close to resembling Julianne. He changed his search requirements to other professions, yet he still found nothing. Jake knew this was going to be harder than he thought. "That's what I get for staring into those beautiful, pleading green eyes," he admonished himself.

He went to get a cup of coffee in the reception area. Donna made a comment about how beautiful Julianne Sullivan was. Jake agreed, but started telling Donna it was going to be difficult finding her father. "I really have nothing to go on," he said.

"If he is as wealthy as she was told he is, maybe at some point he was in the society pages and there would be a picture," Donna said.

A Stranger in the Will

"Donna," Jake said, "that's why I pay you the big bucks." He kissed her on the cheek and went back to his office. "I would have thought of that myself, eventually," Jake laughingly yelled back to Donna as he closed his door.

He sat in his chair and proceeded to bring up Internet society articles for the year. He got to six months ago and sat there staring, eyes wide open, at a picture of Julianne Sullivan in male form. The man's name was Conrad Simms, but it wasn't him that caught his eye, but rather his son Jordan standing next to him. Jordan and Julianne could have been twins. Jake leaned back in his chair, still staring in amazement. He yelled for Donna, wanting confirmation that he wasn't imagining something that wasn't there.

"What are you yelling about?" Donna asked as she entered his office.

"Look at this," Jake said as he pointed to the screen.

Donna, too, stood staring at the picture. "I want a raise for the suggestion," she laughed. "Wow, that's incredible."

"To say the least. Now get out of here, I have work to do." As he began reading the article, concern crossed his face. *Uh-oh, this isn't good*, he thought. As he looked below the picture, the headline read:

**Prominent Los Angeles business-
man Conrad Simms turns over
thriving import/export business
to his son Jordan Simms.
Reports say the elder Simms is in
failing health, but he will**

B. L. Marshall

**continue to be the ruling force as
long as his health permits.**

Jake immediately went to the obituaries from that day to the present and found what he was looking for. Two weeks ago, as big as life, was a picture of the Simms family at Conrad's graveside. The names listed from left to right were: Son, Jordan, daughter, Kylie, wife Madeline and the Simms's family attorney, Christopher Romano. *Well, I guess I have plenty to go on now*, Jake thought. He placed a call to Julianne, asking her how soon she could get there. It was quitting time, but he didn't want to wait until morning. This was a big find.

Having told Jake she could be there in about twenty minutes. Julianne grabbed her purse and room key from the table by the door and headed for her rental car. When she arrived, Donna had left, and Jake met her at the door. "I'm a little nervous," she said. "You sounded concerned over what you found."

"Not so much concerned as amazed. I made copies of the articles I found on your father. Go ahead and have a seat." He pulled out a chair at a small round table.

"I can't believe you found him already. Are you sure you guys aren't friends or something?" She laughed.

"No, I can assure you, we don't run in the same circles. What I found, Julianne, isn't good news. The first thing was a news article of him handing control of his business over to his son Jordan." Jake handed her the copy of that article and waited for her to take it all in. She, too, was amazed at the resemblance to Jordan. She finished reading it, and, while they were her family, she felt bad, but she wasn't heartbroken. She told Jake that, if her father was that sick, she would like to meet him as soon as possible before anything happened to him. On that note, he handed her the copy of the graveside picture, telling her he had already passed. Again, she couldn't be heartbroken, since, she didn't even know him, but she was disappointed that she never would have a chance to get the answers she needed.

"Well, Jake, I guess that's it. I do thank you for finding this information, and I would like copies of those if I may."

"Wait a second, don't you want to meet your half siblings? Perhaps they could fill in the gaps for you."

"Oh, I'm not sure they'd be very receptive. My mother did tell me his children weren't very nice. That would make me nervous."

"Julianne, do you have enough money or a fabulous job waiting for you? Enough of a nest egg or future salary to get you through the rest of your life?"

"No," she said. "I have to decide where I want to settle down and get a job. I have enough money to get to that point, I think."

"Julianne, think about it, you are a legal heir to a fortune. You have a right to your fair share of your father's estate. You would be set for life." Jake was getting hyped up.

"I don't have a birth certificate saying he's my father. I'd be afraid of what his kids would do."

"Listen, that graveside picture lists your father's attorney." He pointed to him. "Why don't we at least pay him a visit and see what he says?"

"Okay, I guess we could do that," she said. But Julianne was hesitant.

"Tomorrow morning I'll call over there and make an appointment to see him. Meanwhile, it's dinnertime. I'm starving, and you don't know anyone, so why don't we go grab a bite before calling it a night? My treat."

"That sounds wonderful. I'm kind of hungry myself," she agreed.

A Stranger in the Will

EIGHT

The next morning Jake called Christopher Romano's office to make the appointment. He didn't want to alert the attorney as to why he wanted to see him, so he told the receptionist he had a client who might be interested in hiring him, which wasn't a total lie. The appointment was made for Friday afternoon at 2:00 p.m. It was Wednesday, so that left him time to prepare for the meeting. It would be interesting, to say the least.

At one o'clock Friday afternoon, Jake picked Julianne up at her hotel, and they headed for Romano's office. Julianne was extremely nervous, not knowing what to expect. Jake tried to calm her down as he told her they were only going to test the waters, not cause the flood. Jake did tell her that Romano was a high-powered attorney, and they were not the type of clientele he is used to seeing walk into his office, so this should be interesting. That didn't help Julianne's composure any.

The receptionist escorted Jake and Julianne into the office. Romano stood, buttoned his expensive suit jacket and extended his hand to greet them. Jake was right, Romano was a little taken aback that he and Julianne's attire was not what he was used to seeing on his clients. There were no visible diamonds or a Rolex.

The trio shook hands as Romano motioned toward an exquisite table along the sidewall under a very large and expensive painting. He looked at Julianne as he tried to figure out how he knew her. The attorney joined them after taking a notepad and pen from his desk.

"What can I do for you, Mr. Matthews, is it?" Again his attention was on Julianne. "Do I know you, miss? You look very familiar."

"No, I assure you we've never met, but please excuse my manners, my name is Julianne Sullivan," she said as she extended her hand to him. At the very mention of that name, Romano went white. He saw Jordan Simms standing before him.

"Mr. Romano, are you all right? Can I get you some water?" Jake asked.

The attorney regained his composure. He got up, walked over to his desk, and brought back a file he got out of a drawer. "Miss Sullivan," he began, "please excuse my reaction, but you are the last person I expected to walk through that door. I know who you are. How did you know to contact me?"

"Hold on a minute." Jake said. "What are you talking about?"

Julianne looked frightened, so Jake took her hand to reassure her it was okay.

Romano began to explain. "Miss Sullivan, you are the child of Conrad Simms and Heather Sullivan, are you not?"

A Stranger in the Will

"Yes, or at least I think Conrad Simms is my father," Julianne said. "My mother never told me who my father was. She didn't want me to have anything to do with him or his family. I never understood why. After she died, I chose to find out for myself, so here I am. I hired Mr. Matthews to find my father, and the pictures he showed me left little question when you look at Jordan."

"You are correct, but how did you know to come to me?"

This time, Jake answered. "Your picture and name were on the graveside photo as the family attorney. I advised Miss Sullivan that she should investigate the possibility of being eligible for a share of the estate."

"Mr. Matthews is right, you are entitled to a portion of your father's estate. As a matter of fact, he had me searching for you in hopes of finding you before the reading of his will, so your arrival is well timed. The reading of the will is scheduled for next Thursday here in my office at 3:30 p. m. His wife, Madeline, and his two children, Jordan and Kylie will also be present. It is my understanding that none of them know anything about you. My suggestion would be for you to stay out of sight until the reading. I advise you not to try to contact them before that. Mr. Matthews, I strongly suggest that you accompany your client when you return on that day.

"It sounds like you're expecting trouble, Mr. Romano," Jake said.

"I don't want to scare you Miss Sullivan, but it would be in your best interest to stay away from Jordan and Kylie. I can't say anymore than that. I'm sure you'll find out for yourself soon enough. This reading will be a real eye opener for all of you. As far as I'm concerned we're finished here until Thursday, unless either of you have any further questions." They all stood, shook hands, and said good-bye for now.

On the drive back to the hotel, Jake could tell Julianne was unsure about what she was doing. Romano had frightened her, and she was not sure she wanted to go through with this. Jake reassured her that everything would be okay. He felt sorry for her that she had a whole week to worry about this and proposed she try to find things to occupy herself. He tried to give her suggestions for touristy things to do. When they got back to her hotel, she thanked him and promised to call if she needed anything.

That night she made some calls to her mom's family in Colorado. She had planned to spend time with them anyway when this business of finding her father was done. Her mother's sister, Carla, talked her into coming for a visit before the reading. Julianne agreed that would help her get though this week a lot easier. The next morning, on the way to the airport, she called Jake's office, and, since it was too early for him and Donna to be there, she left him a message telling him where she was headed and her return information.

A Stranger in the Will

NINE

On Wednesday morning, Julianne said her goodbyes to her aunts, uncles, and cousins, and she sadly left Denver. However sad it was to leave so soon, this way she would have plenty of time to relax and get ready for the reading of her father's will on Thursday. The flight back gave her time to think that perhaps Denver might be one of her choices as to where to settle down when this was all over. It was a beautiful city but, she was not sure of the winters they all spoke of. After living her whole life in Singapore, she couldn't imagine living through a blizzard.

After deplaning in L.A., she walked through the terminal toward baggage claim. She noticed a man standing there, holding a sign with her name on it that obscure his face. She approached the man and announced she was Julianne. Jake dropped the sign and smiled.

"What are you doing here, Jake?"

"I got your message saying when you'd be back, so I thought I'd meet you and we could go to lunch before I take you to your hotel."

"That would be wonderful, thank you." Julianne said.

"Were you able to relax and have a good time with your family?" Jake asked.

"Yes, I had a wonderful time, and we all promised to get together as much as possible."

"That's great, Jake said. "Do you feel you're ready for tomorrow?"

"I don't know. I tried not to think about it. To be honest, I'm rather unsure about doing this."

"Don't you worry about it, I'll be right there with you. I won't let anything happen to you."

After lunch, Jake drove to Julianne's hotel. He walked her inside and up to her room.

"I'll pick you up around three tomorrow. Try to get some sleep." Jake said.

"I'm glad your aunt recommended you Jake," Julianne blushed. "I'll see you tomorrow, you have a good day."

"You too Julianne," Jake replied as he walk away.

Julianne woke the next morning, still quite tired from her trip, along with the fact that she didn't sleep well. She went down to the free breakfast, picked up a paper, and went back to her room. She took her time reading the paper. Realizing she was more nervous than she thought, she tried to stop her hands from shaking as she held the paper. *Okay, stop*, she scolded herself.
You're a grown women, and this is the only way you will get the answers to your questions. Oh mom, she continued. *I know you told me not to do this, and I'm sorry. I hope you understand my need to find out about my dad.* She cried for her mom and the dad she would never know. She fell asleep, but woke in time to shower and have some lunch before Jake was due.

TEN

Jake and Julianne rode to Christopher Romano's office pretty much in silence. The anticipation was controlling both their minds. Jake found a parking spot fairly close to the office. He noticed Julianne was a little shaky, so he took her hand as they went inside. She was hoping they had arrived before the Simms. She thought somehow that would give her the upper hand in the introductions. She soon found out how wrong she was.

Madeline, Kylie, and Jordan walked into Romano's office, and they all shook hands. As they turned to sit at the table Julianne and Jake occupied, Jordan stared. The rage in his eyes told Jake they were in for trouble. Madeline simply asked who these people were, Kylie waited for the fallout.

Romano started the introductions. "Madeline, Jordan, and Kylie Simms, this is Julianne Sullivan and Jake Matthews." No one made a move.

Jordan was livid. "What is she doing here?"

"Jordan, do you know these people?" Madeline asked.

The attorney spoke up. "If everyone will be seated, I'll explain what's going on here."

"Madeline," he began. "Before Conrad died he had me look for Miss Sullivan to have her present for this reading."

"Why, for heaven sake?" She stopped as she turned toward the woman and finally really noticed Julianne. "Oh my God!" She looked at Jordan and back to Julianne. "Don't tell me", she started to say, and trailed off for a moment. "She's Conrad's daughter."

"I'm sorry, Madeline, but yes she is. He met her mother in Singapore. She is a legal heir, and therefore needs to be at this reading."

"Jordan, Kylie, did you know?" Their mother asked.

Jordan said, "Yes, Mother we did. I found out by accident, so I went to Singapore and confronted that slut of a mother. I warned her not to let her daughter pursue this family. I guess she didn't understand my meaning." He said as he glared at Julianne with hatred that couldn't possibly be misunderstood.

Julianne was a raging bull as she stood to confront Jordan. "My mother was not a slut." She was right in Jordan's face. Jake stood and headed toward Jordan just as Jordan reared back and raised his hand toward Julianne. Jake grabbed Jordan's hand and twisted his wrist back. Jordan quickly got Jake's meaning when he noticed the look on his face. He knew he was no physical match against Jake, but he certainly knew how to get in touch with people who were.

The attorney brought a sealed leather binder to the table. "If everyone will sit and control themselves, we can begin." Romano knew there was going to be hell to pay today.

A Stranger in the Will

"No," Jordan shouted, "this will not take place as long as she's sitting here. We don't even know if she is a legal heir." His anger was off the charts.

Romano said, "Jordan before anything left to her in this will can be finalized, she will be required to have DNA testing done. But you can't be serious that you doubt her validity when you look at her."

"I can doubt anything I want. She is not getting anything. I'll see to that!" Jordan shouted.

"Jordan, sit down and be quiet, or you will be the one who is absent during this reading. Your father knew you two," he said, looking at Kylie, "and expected this would be a problem." He left a provision in his will just in case you couldn't be controlled, so I'd be careful if I were you. Now sit down, Jordan."

He reluctantly sat, but kept his glare on Julianne. Jake matched Jordan glare for glare, letting him know that he was ready and willing, anytime"

Romano started by telling Madeline what she was entitled to. Conrad was very generous, but Madeline didn't show any emotion, since she pretty much already knew what Conrad had left her. She kept her eyes on Julianne. Jordan and Kylie were left equal shares in property and monetary bequests. Conrad had already turned the business over to Jordan, but in the will he gave equal shared controlling interest to Kylie and Julianne. This meant Jordan couldn't make any decisions without consulting both of them. He was infuriated, it was plain to see the conniving going on in his mind. *There is no way that was going to happen, positively no way. Julianne wouldn't have anything to do with Simms Trading.*

"Julianne Sullivan, as well as sharing controlling interest in Simms Trading, your father left you the family home on the shores of Lake Tahoe, located at 2643 Mahoney Ct., Incline Village, Nevada, as well as the sum of $2.5 million dollars. That amount is the account balance Conrad put aside to repay your mother for supporting both of you on her own for over 20 years. Since she has passed on, the money is rightfully yours."

"Now, that completes the provisions assigned in his will. In addition, there are rules, as I stated earlier. First Julianne, you must agree to submit to a DNA test. I am to get results before your provisions can be executed. Madeline, Jordan, and Kylie, you all must accept that Julianne is a legal heir to Conrad's estate, or your provisions will be null and void. He also had written a personal letter to you, Madeline, and you, Julianne," he said as he passed a sealed letter to both. Julianne and Jake were in shock as much as Jordan, Kylie, and Madeline were. She never, in a million years, would have thought a father she never met would leave her anything, let alone all that he did. Romano told Julianne she had a week to submit the DNA to him or her inheritance would be null and void.

"That's it," the attorney said. "I'm done. Does anyone have any questions?" No one said anything. Jordan, Kylie, and Madeline all left in a huff. Jake and Julianne shook Romano's hand and thanked him.

"Oh my God," Julianne said. "I can't believe all this."

"Just read your letter, Ms. Sullivan, I think that will answer all your questions."

ELEVEN

On the way back to Julianne's hotel, she laughed, cried, and fidgeted. She couldn't believe what had just happened. Jake just kept looking at her as he smiled.

"I would like you with me while I read this letter. I'm so nervous about what it might say." Julianne said.

"Not a problem." Jake agreed to accompany her upstairs. They got to Julianne's room, but her hands were shaking so badly that Jake had to take the key from her and open the door. Julianne dropped her purse off on the table and asked Jake if he wanted anything to drink. He offered to go to the soda machine down the hall and get them each something. When he came back she was sitting at the table, shadowed by the sunlight. He thought she looked like an angel. Jake handed her the cola he had gotten for her and sat down.

"Whenever you're ready," he said. She looked up at him, waved the letter and let out a sigh. Jake just smiled at her.

"I don't know why I'm so nervous. I don't think I have anymore shock left in me after that reading. Well, here goes," she tore open the letter and shook it out.

It began:

My Dear Julianne,

A Stranger in the Will

As I sit writing this letter, I'm thinking about your mother and the love we shared. I heard she passed away, and my heart broke for such a great loss and because I couldn't be there to help you get through that awful tragedy. I loved her so much. I wish I had been strong enough to stay and make a life with her, and you, my daughter.

I don't know if I can ever make you understand what my motives were when I left her. I know it broke her heart, and I knew she would give birth to you without me there to hold her hand and to hold you for the first time.

I suspect your mother told you I had a family in Los Angles. My two children, however, leave a lot to be desired, as you will find out. I fear my son is capable of anything, so I wanted to keep you and your mother my secret. I feared for your safety, that's why I had to walk away. I can only hope that your mother's strength and determination passed on to you.

You will have to be strong to fight them. Don't let them get the upper hand or hurt you. This is my worst fear. I have no doubt my children will do anything, and I mean anything, to get you out of their way. Please, Julianne, be careful and on your guard at all times.

I wish I didn't have to be talking to you in a letter. I wish I could hug you and tell you how sorry I am that I had to leave, but it was not meant to be. I can tell you, it is a great loss for me. Please remember I thought of you always and hoped you would someday understand why I walked away. It was not because I didn't love you and your mother--it was because I did.

You have my hopes and dreams for a wonderful life. I hope what I have left for you will help get you started toward that goal.

Be careful, my daughter, and God bless.

Much love,
Your Father

Tears were flowing down Julianne's cheeks. Jake handed her a Kleenex, while his own eyes were full, but not overflowing.

"Well," she said, "I guess that at least answered the most important question I had. I wish my mother could have heard this. It would have eased her pain."

"I think she heard." Jake told her.

"That would be nice for her to know he was protecting us by leaving, and that he really did love her." Julianne folded the letter and put it back in the envelope. "I will treasure this always."

"Well," Jake said, "you've had quite a day, Ms. Sullivan. I think it's time I go and let you rest and take it all in. Please call me if you need anything, keep your door locked, and don't go out tonight. Order in your dinner, and make sure it is the hotel staff at the door. I don't trust Jordan. While I don't think he would try anything this soon, you never know. I'll call you later.

"Okay. Thank you so much for being there today and watching over me." She leaned toward him and kissed his cheek, then blushed.

Jake responded by saying, "Good night pretty lady." He didn't trust himself to return the kiss, even if it was just on her cheek.

TWELVE

Meanwhile, Madeline was sitting in the privacy of her bedroom, getting ready to read her own personal note from Conrad. She was crying as she remembered her heart tried to keep beating, the moment she realized who the stranger was sitting across the table in Christopher Romano's office. She stood and went to her desk to get her letter opener. As she sat in her favorite chair by the window, she began to read.

My Dear Madeline,

If you're reading this you have already met my daughter, Julianne. I know it will be difficult for you to hear what I am about to say, but please bear with me.

I know it is the oldest excuse in the world, I never meant for it to happen!, but it's the truth. I certainly was not looking to have an affair, it just landed at my feet. I have always loved you from the day we met and will until the day I die. I can only hope you believe that. I tried to show you all the years we were together.

When Julianne's mother told me she was pregnant, I did a terrible thing and walked out on her. I never spoke to her again. I won't lie to you,

A Stranger in the Will

I loved her too. I never knew you could love two very different people equally. I knew my life was here, so I broke the heart of my unborn child's mother. My affair had nothing to do with any problems with you. I didn't feel misunderstood or denied of your love. It was all me.

When I found out I only had months to live, I had Christopher Romano help me find Julianne. We found her mother had passed away and that my daughter was left alone. That's when I knew I had to meet her and provide for her as I would Jordan and Kylie. It's getting very close to the end now, and I haven't met her yet. I fear I will run out of time, and I will never see that happen.

It is a terrible thing to say, but my greatest fear is that Jordan and Kylie will try to harm Julianne. We have raised two very selfish and malicious children, and I will go to my grave ashamed. I know you know that as well. Please try to talk to them and make them understand that this is not Julianne's fault. I pray you can get through to them before they do something they'll regret.

I will go to my grave with many regrets, one being that you seeing Julianne has hurt you deeply. I am so sorry, and I know you can't forgive me, but please help stop our children from making the mistake of their lives. I hope you will meet someone else who can love you the way you deserved to be loved. Please don't judge any suitor by my actions. I hope someday you will realize how much I really did and do love you.

B. L. Marshall

Conrad

Madeline tried very hard not to tear the letter up and throw it in her fireplace. She knew what he said about their children was true. She knew deep down inside that especially Jordan would be apt to do something very stupid. His outrageous behavior in Romano's office was frightening and only a small sample of his temper. Madeline stashed the letter in her desk drawer then headed for the living room.

She found Jordan and Kylie out by the pool. When she approached them they stopped their discussion. Jordan held up the drink in his hand as he asked if she would like one. "No thank you," she replied, "but I would like to know what you two were plotting, and don't try to deny you were. I heard enough anger in your tone, Jordan, to know something isn't right. If it has anything to do with Julianne, we need to talk. I just read the letter your father left for me. He explained about his affair with her mother. I'm not stupid, I know how those things can happen. He did tell me that he loved both of us, but he chose to walk away and come back home. That being said, he asked that I have a talk with both of you about Julianne. I'm telling you right now, you leave her alone. I will have our attorney talk to her about giving up the controlling interest in Simms Trading, but the money and the Tahoe house will remain hers. You have got to accept the fact that she is his daughter, and it's only right that he provide for her as he did both of you."

A Stranger in the Will

"Mom, they never even knew each other, and she is illegitimate. How does that make her an heir?" Jordan asked.

"Jordan, regardless of how you feel about this, she is your father's daughter. He wanted to do this for her to repay her in some way for not being there for her. She's twenty-two years old and never had a chance to know her father."

"Big deal," Jordan said, "I imagine there are thousands of kids that never knew their fathers and I'm sure they didn't get a house and money. Mother, she knows nothing about Simms Trading, she has no right to be involved in that."

"I agree with that, Jordan, and I said I will talk to Christopher Romano about that part, but both of you have to promise you will stay away from her." Madeline insisted.

"Okay," Kylie said, "I won't bother her."

Madeline looked at Jordan, waiting for an answer. "Jordan?"

"I'll give you my answer after we pay Christopher a visit. "I'm sorry, Mother, I just can't accept any of this." He got up and walked away.

"Kylie, you have to promise me you'll tell me if Jordan is going to try to go after Julianne." Kylie just stood and looked at her mother, then jumped in the pool without answering her.

Oh my Lord, Madeline thought, *it's already out of control. Damn you, Conrad, why did you leave me with this?.*

Madeline picked up the phone and called Romano's office. She told his receptionist it was imperative she speak with him no later than tomorrow. The receptionist gave her a phone appointment for 4:30 tomorrow afternoon.

Meanwhile, Jordan was very busy trying to find the hotel where Julianne was registered. He told Kylie he was planning on getting someone to go after her before she had a chance to go get the DNA done.

THIRTEEN

Julianne woke to a knock at her door. She threw her robe on and looked through the peep hole. There stood Jake with a bag in his hand and newspaper under his arm. Julianne secured her robe. She smiled as she opened the door. "What are you doing here so early, Jake? I'm a mess. What time is it anyway?"

"Well, sleepy head, it's nine o'clock, and you're far from a mess. I was going to call first, but I was sure you'd be up. I brought us some breakfast and the paper. I was concerned you might try to go out for breakfast, and I didn't want you doing that."

"Jake, do you really think Jordan will try something? I mean isn't he the first one they would look at if something happened to me?"

"Yes, I'm sure he would be, but he won't do anything himself. He's not that stupid. Last night I couldn't sleep, my mind was going constantly. The one thing that came out of that was, if Jordan wanted to cause you harm, I would think he would try before it could be proved that you are Conrad Simms's daughter. Meaning, before you have that DNA test done."

"Wow, this could be right out of a crime series on TV. Maybe if I go do the DNA testing today and get it right over to Christopher Romano, I will have taken away his need to do anything. How about that? Two can play this game."

"Julianne, first off, this is not a game, he's dead serious. And second, I don't think it'll stop him. He won't stop until he's sure you're not getting anything that he feels belongs to them. But in regards to your idea, getting it over with today could slow him down a bit. It certainly would take away the urgency to keep you from proving you're Conrad's daughter. Too late...." Jake smiled.

"Okay, let's eat this breakfast, that smells so good. Then, you can read the paper while I shower and get ready. I have to find the paperwork the attorney gave me to see where I go to get the test done. He said I didn't need an appointment." Julianne replied.

When Julianne was ready they left the hotel and went to the lab assigned to do the DNA. She was told by the technician that the results would go to Romano's office by the next day. Previous arrangements had been made to put a rush on it, the lab had been paid handsomely to provide that service.

Julianne and Jake returned to her hotel. Jake was going to drop her off but thought it better he make sure she got to her room okay.

As they passed by the reception desk, the clerk stopped her. "Ms. Sullivan, I thought you should know that another clerk got a call a little while ago. A man was asking if you were registered here." Julianne looked at Jake. The clerk pointed at Jake. "This gentleman here had put a note on your room not to tell anyone you were staying here. However, the girl who answered the phone is fairly new, and she told the caller she was not at liberty to say, instead of saying no. I'm sure that told him what he wanted to know. I'm so sorry."

Jake told the clerk to get her check out bill ready, they were going up to her room to pack her things. He looked at Julianne and said, "You're moving to another hotel."

In her room, Julianne began to hurriedly pack her things, trying to make sure she didn't forget anything. While Jake was watching her he had an idea but wasn't sure she would go for it.

"Julianne," I'm going to suggest something to you, and please hear me out before you answer." She stopped and sat on the edge of the bed, looking at him. "I don't know if you noticed when you came to my office, but it's a two story house. My office occupies the whole downstairs, and I live upstairs. There are two bedrooms and two bathrooms. I would feel much better about all this if you would come and stay there. I can ensure your safety better there than when I'm so far away from you, and I promise I will be a perfect gentleman."

"Oh Jake, that is so nice, but I wouldn't feel comfortable putting you and Donna in any danger should Jordan come after me. I think if I go to another hotel, he'll have to start over again looking for me and that will take time."

"I'm not going to pressure you, but the invitation is there if you change your mind."

"You know, Jake. I hired you to find my father, and you have already done that. I didn't mean for you to get involved in all the rest of this. I am grateful you went with me to the attorney's office, but I don't want you or Donna getting hurt because you got involved."

"Julianne, you don't have anyone else here, and I'm not going to walk away and leave you to fend for yourself against that kind of money and power. I want to make sure you stay safe until this is over, no matter how long that takes. I have done some checking on Jordan, and he is not someone to mess with. I didn't tell you before because I wasn't sure how definite the information was, but I found evidence of a trip he took to Singapore around the time your mother was dying. I don't doubt for one minute that he paid her a visit. Why else would he go there? The business your father had there was done a year or so ago. He was there six months ago and only overnight."

"You're kidding." Julianne looked deep in thought for a minute and then said, "That must be why my mother was so scared about me looking for my father. He must have threatened her, but how did he find her? Also, she was adamant that I not pursue any relationship with him or his family. Whenever she mentioned it I could see the fear in her eyes, but she never admitted anything."

"If Jordan could find her when your father kept her a secret, then he can find you. I wish you would reconsider my suggestion to stay at my place."

"One night in a new hotel will give me time to think about it, I'll let you know tomorrow, fair enough?"

"Okay," Jake said. "I'd rather not, but if that's the best I'm going to get, I'll take it."

A Stranger in the Will

FOURTEEN

Julianne was checking into her new hotel, with Jake by her side, while Jordan's "associate" was outside waiting for Jake to leave.

Ivan, Jordan's "bad boy for hire," had been waiting for Julianne to come out or go into the hotel where Jordan was sure she was registered. He sighed as he saw Julianne and Jake enter the hotel, he called Jordan to inform him, and asked if he was to stay on her or leave for now. Jordan told him to stay put until the P.I. left, find out what room she was in, and pay her a visit.

"Don't hurt her yet, just scare the hell out of her. Then, hopefully, she'll leave without pursuing this any further."

Ivan said, "With all your father left her, you really think she would walk away from it?"

"That's not for you to worry about, Ivan. If your visit doesn't work, I'll have to decide what to do next."

"Okay boss," Ivan replied as he hung up. Ivan spotted both of them coming back out of the hotel, carrying her bags. *Ah*, Ivan said to himself, *where are you going now, little lady*? He followed them to the new hotel and notified Jordan. Jordan told him to hold tight and stay with the original plan.

Ivan was getting a bit antsy. He'd been waiting a couple of hours since they checked into the new hotel and was tired of waiting for the P.I. to leave. He got out of the car and went inside to see what he could find out. While he was standing at the reception desk, he saw them coming out of the dining room. *Oh nice*, he said to himself. I'm outside starving while they're having dinner. The desk clerk was waiting for him to say something instead of watching the pretty girl walk passed.

"Sir?" The clerk finally said. "Can I help you?"

"Yes, I'm sorry. I need to know Ms. Julianne Sullivan's room number please. I have papers here. He showed the clerk an empty manila envelope. "I need her to sign them right away."

"You were just staring at her, sir. She just got on the elevator." The clerk said.

"Oh, that pretty lady that just went by? I never met her. I'm just delivery for the law firm so I didn't know that was her. If you tell me which room she's in, I'll take care of this now."

"I'm sorry sir, I'm not allowed to give out her room number. If you want to wait while she has time to get to her room, I can call and ask if it's okay to send you up."

"That would be fine," Ivan said as he watched the elevator stop on the 4th floor. He waited right by the clerk as he called Julianne's room. He purposely watched for the room number the clerk punched into the phone.

"They must have stopped to enjoy the atrium before going to her room, there's no answer yet." The clerk reported.

"That's okay. I'll be back in about a half an hour. I have another document that needs to be signed tonight, so I'll go do that one first and come back," Ivan said as he walked away.

A Stranger in the Will

Jake exited the hotel, not very happy that he left Julianne there alone. *She's a stubborn one*, he said to himself as he got into his car.

Ivan perked up when he saw Jake exit the hotel. *Finally*, he thought, *now I can get this done and go home*. Ivan walked into the hotel lobby behind someone else, making sure the clerk that waited on him didn't see him. Much to Ivan's surprise, the clerk wasn't even at the desk. He headed to the bank of elevators and pushed the up button. He had gone home and changed into a very nice business suit. He had to look the part so Julianne wouldn't be suspicious when she looked out the peephole. The elevator doors opened on the 4th floor. Ivan looked up and down the hall, and, when he didn't see anyone, he walked to room 425 and knocked on the door.

"Who is it?" Julianne inquired.

"Ms. Sullivan, my name is Robert Fenton. I'm here with some papers for you to sign from Christopher Romano's office." Julianne looked out the peephole. She saw a man dressed in a very nice suit holding up a manila envelope. With what had gone on tonight, she wasn't about to open the door. She told him she was not aware of any papers being sent over by Mr. Romano, and that he should have called her about it.

"Sorry miss, I'm just delivery. It'll only take a minute."

"You take them back to the office and tell Mr. Romano I will be in tomorrow morning to sign them. It's a little late tonight." While Ivan was trying to convince her to open the door and sign them, she was dialing Jake's cell phone. She figured he just left a few minutes ago, so he couldn't be far away. Jake answered his phone and immediately heard the distress in Julianne's voice. He didn't even wait for her to explain before he pulled into the nearest spot where he could turn around and headed back to the hotel. Julianne told him about the man at the door. Jake felt a chill crawl up his spine, and he knew this was not a good thing.

"Julianne, call the front desk and have security come up. It'll probably take me 4 to 5 minutes to get there. Try to keep him talking outside the door until someone comes."

"Okay," she said.

"Hold on another minute, I'm getting dressed," she yelled towards the door.

Ivan was leaning against the wall when the elevator doors opened. Two security guards exited and started walking toward him. He turned, looked for the stairwell, spotted the exit sign, and bolted. The two guards were in pursuit down the stairs, as Ivan ducked into the hall a couple of floors down. People were just getting off the elevator, so he jumped on and hit the lobby button. He was gone.

A Stranger in the Will

FIFTEEN

As Jake came to a screeching halt in front of the hotel, Ivan was calling Jordan to tell him he never got the chance to talk to Julianne. He explained what happened. He could hear the anger coming through the phone when Jordan began to speak.

"Well," Jordan said, "you didn't handle that very well, did you? Was that too much for you, Ivan? Do I trust you will handle the next one better, or should I put someone else on this?"

"I can handle it just fine," Ivan said with an attitude, "It wasn't my fault she called security. I did everything okay, but if you want to get someone else, you go right ahead. I don't need this hassle from you." Ivan was irate over Jordan's accusations.

"Okay, I apologize. I just got really frustrated for a minute. I'll call you later when I put together another plan." He told Ivan he had to get to her before she had the DNA test done. As he hung up, Jordan's phone rang. He was about to be told the news that Julianne was indeed Conrad's daughter. The DNA had been verified already.

Jake hurried to Julianne's room. As he knocked on her door, he called out her name. Julianne opened the door, and threw herself into his arms. She was still shaking over the whole ordeal. Jake held on tight, rubbing her back as he whispered in her ear that everything was okay now. He had a hard time concentrating, the smell of her hair and her perfume was sending signals through his body he hadn't felt in a very long time. However, he knew he didn't have time for that now, so his mind was racing to come up with something to say. "Julianne," he finally asked, "do you know if security caught up with him?"

"No, they didn't. They called here after they chased him. They said he got away and to lock every lock on the door. They would keep an eye out around the hotel."

"Did you already unpack your bags? If not get them and gather the things you have already taken out. You're out of here." Julianne didn't hesitate this time. When they finished packing her things, they checked her out.

The hotel waived the charges for the few hours she was there as a gesture of good faith because of her horrible experience. She and Jake thanked them and headed toward Jake's car.

"What about my rental car?" Julianne asked.

"We'll pick it up tomorrow," Jake replied. As he drove, he was checking the rear view mirror constantly to make sure no one was following. He even took the long way around, just to be sure. It bothered him, he wondered how they knew she switched hotels. The only thing he came up with was Jordan must have already had someone stationed outside the first hotel after the clerk as much as told him Julianne was there.

Jake knew this was serious. Jordan had started sooner than he thought he would. He looked across the seat at Julianne. His heart ached knowing that Jordan's obsession with getting her out of the picture was just beginning. He vowed at that very moment that he would protect Julianne with his life.

When they arrived at his place, the whole house was in darkness. Jake opened the door to the office and put Julianne in a dark corner so she would be hidden while he checked the whole bottom floor. "All clear," he whispered. "Now the upstairs, you stay put, and I'll come down and get you when I'm sure it's okay." Julianne nodded her head.

She was getting nervous, for it seemed to be taking an awful long time. All of the sudden she heard footsteps bounding rapidly down the stairs. She knew deep in her bones that it wasn't Jake.

She squatted further into the corner and held her breath. A large dark figure passed by her as he ran out the door. She waited in case there was someone else, but wanted desperately to go up to make sure Jake was okay. Finally she heard Jake coming down.

"Julianne, are you okay?"

"Yes I'm all right, but what happened?" She saw Jake come around the corner, holding his head. She noticed a bit of blood running from his nose.

"Are you all right?"

"Yeah, he came out from behind the shower curtain. He shoved me aside, and I fell into the mirror, nose first. I'll be okay." Jake took his gun from his desk drawer and went outside to look around. No one was there. He grabbed Julianne's things from the trunk and went back inside. He locked up and swore he would get an alarm system put in tomorrow. He took Julianne's bags to her room and showed her around the whole apartment.

"Listen, I have locked the place up tight, but that didn't stop him from getting in, so here's the deal. I'm going to need your help until the alarm system gets put in. We're going to have to take turns staying awake and listening. You choose whether you want to sleep first. We've both been up a long time, but I've still got some time left in me."

"You really think he would try again tonight?" she asked. "I wish I knew."

"You've got a sectional sofa, we can each fit at opposite ends. Why don't we both sleep out here tonight? One of us surely would hear the door," Julianne suggested.

"Beautiful and clever, that's a dangerous combo," Jake laughed, and Julianne blushed.

SIXTEEN

The sun came up as Jake slept on the sun's receiving end of the sectional. He squinted and, looked at his watch. Julianne stirred a bit, asking what time it was.

"You rest a few more minutes while I take a quick shower, then I'll fix us some breakfast while you shower. If you want, you can spend the day unpacking and arranging the room the way you want it. I'll be working downstairs most of the day. I do have an appointment at one o'clock, but Donna will be here. Also, I'm going to call a friend of mine and ask him if he can come over for those couple hours I'll be gone. His name is Nick, he's an L.A. cop out on medical leave for another couple of weeks," Jake explained.

"How convenient."

"I'll be out shortly," Jake said. "There are two bathrooms, but I think it would be better for one of us to be out here or downstairs at all times, for today anyway."

Julianne couldn't get back to sleep, so she made herself at home. She made coffee, poured juice, then went to straighten the blankets on the sofa. Jake stepped out of the shower and immediately smelled the coffee. *I think this will work out just fine. Maybe too fine*, he thought, the idea making him smile. When he walked into the kitchen, Julianne was having a cup of coffee. She saw him and hung her head a little to hide her mussed up hair and the makeup smeared on her face.

"I should have washed my face last night," she said. Jake barely heard her because, he was so taken by how beautiful she was, even in the morning. He was beginning to scare himself with all these thoughts about her. It had been a long time since any woman turned him on like she did.

She left him to make breakfast while she cleaned up. The room was cozy and just right for her. She was beginning to think maybe Jake was too. Then she thought that was a stupid idea, what on earth would he want with a handful of trouble. He had enough of that already in his line of work. She dismissed the idea and headed for the bathroom. When she was finished it was her turn to smell the wonderful smells of breakfast cooking. As she entered the kitchen, she stood in the doorway for a minute, taking in Jake standing at the stove flipping pancakes. It was a wonderful sight.

He turned and caught her looking at him. She had a bit of a sexy smile on her face, and his body started doing that thing again. Now it was his turn to blush.

"I hope you like pancakes," he said.

"I love 'em, and those look fantastic. I'm hungry."

"Well have a seat and dig in," Jake said as he flipped a couple on her plate. When they were done eating, Julianne told Jake to go downstairs and get to work. She would clean up.

"WOW, you better be careful. I could get used to this," Jake said as he opened the door. "I'll

A Stranger in the Will

come up when we're ready to order lunch. Give some thought as to what you'd like."

When Donna came in, Jake told her what happened last night and that Julianne would be staying upstairs in the spare room for awhile. Donna asked him what he was going to do about Jordan.

"First things first," he said. He asked her to call an alarm company and get them over there as soon as possible. He wanted the whole place wired. Next, he asked her to get his friend Nick on the phone for him. A little while later Donna stood in Jake's office doorway, leaning in to tell him the alarm company couldn't come until tomorrow. "None of them could make it today," she informed him, and Nick said he'd call you right back. He was in the middle of something."

"Shit," Jake said. "I was hoping to get an alarm installed today."

"Jake, even if they come tomorrow you won't get it installed probably for a day or two," Donna told him.

"I can't do that. Julianne's safety is at stake here."

"I know it's none of my business, but what were you thinking bringing her here?"

"Where else was she going to go? We tried changing hotels, and they followed us. They almost got to her. This is the only place I can keep her safe."

"Jake, what's going on here? She only hired you to find her father. You did that. You should be done."

"Donna, what do you think I should do? Jordan Simms has his sights set on her. He as much as threatened Julianne right there in front of all of us! After last night, I would say he meant what he said. I can't just cut her loose to fend for herself."

"Jake, I can understand you wanting to help, but bodyguard is a bit outside of your expertise. Or isn't that the only reason you're doing this?"

Jake was saved by the bell when Nick called back. His friend agreed to help him out, and said he'd be there around 12:30 p.m.

Donna went to pick up their lunch at 11:30 a.m. While she was gone Jake made a call to Jordan Simms. Of course Jordan denied knowing anything about what was going on, but Jake gave him fair warning anyway.

The day went by without incident. Jake locked up and headed upstairs. He explained to Julianne that they would have the same sleeping arrangement tonight unless she would rather do shifts tonight. He also told her about his call to Jordan, that got him nowhere.

"I got a call today myself," she said. "Christopher Romano's office called on my cell, and he wants me to come to his office tomorrow at 3:30 p. m. to finalize my part of the will."

"Okay, we can do that."

"Jake, I feel so bad that you have to change everything around to take me somewhere. Why don't I call for a car and go alone. Nobody will know the car and none of the Simms will be there for this anyway."

A Stranger in the Will

"Not a chance. You don't think with all the years Romano has been their attorney they couldn't find out anything they wanted to? His secretary or receptionist or fellow attorney in the office, probably all have Jordan on speed dial." He took her shoulders in his hands. "Listen to me. Until this is all over, I am your shadow. These people don't play nice, but nobody is going to hurt you. Julianne, you have every right to your share of Conrad Simms's estate, and obviously your father thought so, too. Jordan isn't going to take that away from you. Now that that's settled, let's see what I have around here to make for dinner." They ate on TV trays while watching the news and chose to share the sectional again. Jake was happy when they woke the next morning and had not had any unwanted visitors.

SEVENTEEN

At 2:30 that afternoon, Jake closed up his office and told Donna he was taking Julianne to the attorney's office for her appointment. He wasn't sure what time they'd be back so he told her to just lock up, leave some lights on, and have a good night.

At about 4:00 p.m. a man walked into Jake's agency. Donna asked what she could do for him.

"I'd like to speak to Jake Matthews," he said.

"I'm sorry, sir. Jake is not here right now. Can I make an appointment for you for tomorrow?"

"When will he be back?" he asked.

"I'm not sure Mr. ...?" There was no reply. "He had an appointment at 3:30 p.m. " Donna was beginning to get a bad feeling about this guy. She tried to get him to make an appointment, but he wasn't even listening to her. He headed towards Jake's office and opened the door.

"You can't go in there." Donna got up and walked over to close the door. Suddenly, Ivan backhanded her across the face. She fell backwards hitting the back of her head on the file cabinet. She momentarily saw stars and fought not to pass out. Ivan continued up the stairs. Once again she yelled that he couldn't go up there. Ivan tried the door, but it was locked. He came back down.

"Where's the key, bitch?"

"I don't have one," Donna said.

A Stranger in the Will

"Is she up there now?" Ivan asked.

"Who's she?" Donna replied.

"You know who I'm talking about," Ivan said as he pulled her up by the hair and backhanded her again. This time he hit her so hard he knocked her out, so he let her drop to the floor. He searched her desk for Jake's key to the upstairs apartment. When he didn't find it he thought his time was running out. Jake would probably be back anytime. He stepped over Donna and left.

Jake and Julianne's appointment was rather long. Going over all the legalities and signing all the various papers took quite awhile. When they were done, Romano handed her a check for the $2.5 million dollars Conrad had left her, along with the keys and deed to the house in Lake Tahoe. He told her when she reported to work Jordan would give her the key to Simms Trading.

Jake spoke up and said, "I don't think Jordan's going to be forthcoming. We think he hired someone to get to Julianne and convince her to drop all this, or worse. We have already had two incidents where a stranger has tried to get to her."

"Can you prove it has anything to do with Jordan? Not that I doubt that, since he is capable of anything. I believe your father told you that in his letter to you, Julianne," Romano stated.

"I can't prove it yet, but I will," Jake said.

"You keep me posted, Jake. You heard me warn them the day you were all here for the reading. If he and Kylie cause any trouble, they could lose everything Conrad left them."

Right after Jake and Julianne left the attorney's office, a call came in from Madeline Simms.

"Good afternoon, Madeline," Romano said. "What can I do for you?"

"Christopher, I promised Jordan I would call and ask you to intervene on our behalf with Julianne to see if she would be willing to at least give up the controlling interest in Simms Trading. He can deal with the rest of it, although he is still seething."

"Madeline, I am sorry, but Julianne just left here. She has already signed the papers and received everything she was entitled to."

"But, could you still talk to her to see if she would be willing?"

"I can ask, but that's about it. I'll give her time to deal with what she just did here, then I'll call her and ask."

"Thank you so much, Christopher. I just want to ward off any problems between her and Jordan. I'll wait for your call." She hung up.

He wanted to tell Madeline what he'd just heard from Jake and Julianne. Unfortunately, Romano knew that, without proof, such an accusation would only put Julianne in more danger.

Jake pulled into the parking lot after they had stopped for dinner. He knew right away that something wasn't right. The office was still blazing with light. He told Julianne to wait in the car. Donna should have left a couple of hours ago, but her car was still in the lot.

"Jake, why don't you call the police? It might not be safe to go in there."

A Stranger in the Will

"Use your cell and call them," he told Julianne.

"Jake!" She yelled, but he was already inside with his gun drawn.

"Julianne," he yelled from inside, "tell them we need an ambulance as well. It's Donna!"

"Oh God!" Julianne's hands were shaking while she dialed the phone as she was running into the office. "Is she alive, Jake?"

Jake was staring at Donna's bloodied, swollen and bruised face. "Donna, Donna," he kept saying, trying to gently shake her. She let out a moan, and Jake's eyes filled.

Julianne was at the brink of hysteria, she knew it was her fault this happened. She made up her mind right there that she was leaving as soon as she knew Donna would be okay.

The police arrived as the EMT's were checking Donna. They inserted an IV, gave her pain medication, and transported her to the hospital. Jake didn't even get a chance to find out what happened, but he was pretty sure he already knew.

The police had Jake check around to see if anything was missing. He said "no," but he did notice all the keys scattered around. He knew someone was looking for the apartment key. When the police were finished, Jake locked up. He and Julianne headed for the hospital to be with Donna.

EIGHTEEN

Jake and Julianne arrived at the hospital and checked in at the ER. The nurse informed them the doctor was still in with Donna, but she was conscious and talking.

"Thank God," Jake said. "When can we see her?" The nurse went to ask. When she returned she asked them to follow her. They saw Donna lying on the bed. It was more than they could bear. A heart wrenching feeling flowed through both of them. Julianne walked to her bedside and told her how sorry she was that her being there had put her in danger. Donna squeezed her hand, trying to convey to Julianne that she didn't blame her. Jake was on the other side of the bed holding Donna's other hand. She tried to talk to him, but it was too painful.

"Never mind," Jake said. "We'll talk it all out later. I'll get him, Donna. I promise."

The doctor came in, told them he ordered tests to make sure there were no injuries to her head or facial bone structure that he was not seeing. "The technician will be in shortly to take you down, and I'll see you after the results come back." Donna tried to shake her head to show she understood, but couldn't. When the tech came in, Jake told Donna that he and Julianne would be in the waiting room when she came back.

As Donna was being wheeled away, Jake couldn't hold back the tears that had pooled in his

A Stranger in the Will

eyes. Julianne took his hand, and he turned to let her hold him.

It took about 45 minutes for the tests. The nurse came to get them when Donna was back in the ER. She was asleep, so they sat with her until the doctor came in with the results.

"Donna," The doctor said, "I have your test results." She opened her eyes, and he told her that everything looked fine. "Good news, no broken bones or head trauma. You were lucky, there were only superficial cuts and bruises. We are keeping you for a couple of days so we can take care of the wounds and control the pain, but you should recover just fine." Jake thanked the doctor, shook his hand, and turned back to Donna.

"That's wonderful news," Jake said as he kissed her hand. "We'll go now and let you sleep. I'll see you tomorrow. Maybe we can get a description of the man who did this and can talk about what happened then." She squeezed *his* hand this time.

On the ride home Julianne said, "My God, what have I done? I should have listened to my mother. I think I should leave tomorrow and go back to Singapore, and forget all this."

Jake looked over at her. She was talking to his reflection while looking out the window.

"Julianne, you didn't do this to Donna. This is Jordan's doing, not yours. Somebody has to stop him. It won't matter if you leave. I'll still go after him for what he did to her. Your leaving won't stop anything."

Just then Julianne's phone rang. "Ms. Sullivan, this is Christopher Romano. I have a request from

Madeline Simms to relay to you. If you have a minute, we can do this over the phone.

"Okay," Julianne said. She put him on speaker so Jake could hear as well.

"Mrs. Simms called shortly after you left today and asked that I intervene on the family's behalf. They want to know if you would be willing to forfeit your controlling interest in Simms Trading? The rest of your inheritance would remain the same. I explained that you had just left and all the paperwork had been completed, but she requested I ask anyway. Is that something you wouldn't mind doing, or were you hoping to make a career for yourself there?"

Jake swung the car into a parking lot so he could concentrate on the conversation instead of driving.

"Christopher, this is Jake. We had another attack today, this one against my secretary. Someone came in and used her as a punching bag. We stopped for dinner after our meeting with you, so we were late getting back. They were looking for Julianne."

"I'm so sorry Jake. Will she be okay?"

"She will recover, but she's pretty bad right now. If I find this is Jordan's doing, there will be no place he can hide, you can be assured of that."

"Jake, you let the police handle it so no one else gets hurt."

Julianne interrupted. "Listen, Christopher, I will let you know my answer tomorrow. Jake and I have some talking to do tonight. I can't think right now."

A Stranger in the Will

"Understandable, Julianne, we'll talk tomorrow. Good night." The line went dead.

Jake told Julianne that the alarm company wasn't coming until tomorrow, which meant they would have to sleep on the sofa again tonight. "I have an idea though, until the alarm is put in tomorrow, why don't we get adjoining rooms at a hotel for tonight? That way we can both get some much needed sleep. I'm just not sure it's safe to go back to the office tonight."

"That's fine with me. It would be nice to sleep in a bed and not be afraid. As a matter of fact, why don't we just stop at a store and buy everything we need so we don't have to go back to the apartment at all tonight?"

"Great idea," Jake said.

They woke the next morning feeling better, physically anyway. It was wonderful sleeping in a bed, even if they both tossed all night worrying about Donna. Wondering what was coming next.

NINETEEN

Jake suggested they go for breakfast then head back to the office. They would have some cleaning up to do. Julianne asked if they should call the police and have them meet them there. Jake told her he had already called his friend Nick, and he would be there.

"That's good," Julianne said. "Jake, I'm so sorry about all this, I never thought..." she trailed off as Jake put his finger over her lips.

"Don't you even say it. I already told you this is Jordan's doing, not yours."

"All I'm saying is that if I had never come here, none of this would be happening, and Jordan wouldn't be such a raving lunatic."

"From what I've found about him, he's a raving lunatic anyway. Look, let's just get the office straightened out. I'm going to have to get a temp in here until we know what's going on with Donna."

"I can stay for awhile and help do Donna's work," Julianne said. "That's what I did in Singapore.""It's the least I can do, Jake."

"Oh yeah, I can see that. A millionaire working as a temp. Besides, I don't want you out in the open like that."

"I'd rather do it than put a temp in harm's way. That would give you a hell of a reputation for hiring future temps if this happened again. Maybe you could get Nick to accept a temp job as security here until he returns to work or Jordan is stopped." She raised her eyebrows, waiting for Jake's response. She thought it was a damn good idea.

"That would be an excellent idea, except my business is not that hot right now. I don't have the money to pay Nick, you, and keep paying Donna. She was injured while working for me, so I feel I need to keep up her salary and health insurance. She and her husband struggle as it is. It wouldn't be right to cut her off, that would be like cutting off my right arm."

"Jake, that is the nicest thing I have ever heard. You are an extraordinary person, but I didn't ask for a salary. I'm paying you to protect me, and you would be right here, or Nick would be.

"You're embarrassing me, "Jake laughed. "All kidding aside, I don't know how I would survive around here without her. She's been with me since the opening of the agency. Enough of this! It's depressing. Are you ready to go and get started with the clean up? We'll talk later."

"Let's hit it," Julianne said. Nick showed up, and the trio got busy picking up all the papers, keys, and plants. Jake looked around and surveyed his property. The alarm company was due in an hour, so they locked up the office and went upstairs for coffee. Nick asked Jake what he was going to do without Donna for probably quite awhile.

"I don't know," Jake replied. "I'm not busy right now, so Julianne and I could probably handle things."

"You just finished a big case," Julianne said. "Now I'm your only client, right?"

"Well, that went through the heart," Jake said.

"I didn't mean it like that. My point is, since you don't have anything pressing right now, why don't you and I go check out the place in Lake Tahoe to get away for awhile. I'm paying you to protect me anyway, but if you feel there would be trouble up there, I would pay Nick to be extra protection if he would like to go for a few days. What do you guys think?"

"Hey, I would love to stay on Lake Tahoe for a few days," Nick said. "Jake it would be fun, we can water ski and Jet Ski. The water would be very therapeutic for my recovery," Nick laughed.

"It would be nice to get away from all this. It's certainly been very stressful," Jake admitted.

"It's settled then. I'll call Christopher Romano and tell him I'll give him my decision about Simms Trading when we get back. I need to think it through. I don't want to be too hasty. So Nick, you're in?"

"You betcha."

"When do we leave?" Jake asked.

"Tomorrow morning sounds good to me. How about you guys?" Julianne asked.

"Okay, I'll meet you here at ten tomorrow morning and away we'll go," Nick said.

"Thanks for all your help, buddy," Jake was saying as the bell rang. "Must be the alarm guys."

Nick shook Jake's hand while assuring him again, that he'd be here by ten in the morning.

"Don't leave without me," he teased. Then he left.

A Stranger in the Will

It took about an hour for the alarm company to give Jake an estimate and a time they could install it. The deal was made for Monday next week. They would plan to be back from Tahoe by then.

Jake looked for Julianne to tell her he wanted to stop by the hospital before they left in the morning. He wanted to tell Donna what was going on and to assure her she had nothing to worry about, as he would see that she was taken care of.

He found her on the phone holding for Romano to tell him they were going up to check out the house in Tahoe and that she would call him with her decision when she got back. Romano finally answered and agreed she needed the time away.

Erin, Romano's receptionist, was in his office while he was talking to Julianne on speakerphone. She returned to her desk to immediately phone Jordan. She had an expensive lifestyle to maintain and being Romano's receptionist just wasn't enough. Jordan had approached her years ago about being his snitch so he would know what his dad was doing with business issues. Erin, was the one, who blew the whistle on Heather and Julianne Sullivan in Singapore.

Nick showed up at 10 a.m. sharp the following morning. He was packed and ready to head out. When he pulled in the parking lot, he noticed a car sitting around the corner, the driver inside. His cop sense immediately kicked in. He went inside to tell Jake. They decided to go out the back and approach the vehicle from behind to check it out.

They agreed that Nick would knock on the driver's side window while Jake stayed back a little on the passenger's side, just in case he was needed. Nick tapped on the window, which startled the very large man in the driver's seat. He was dressed in black, and Nick also noticed a ski mask on the passenger's seat. Ivan rolled down the window, acting completely calm and innocent. "What is it?" Ivan asked.

"What are you doing out here besides watching that house?" Nick pointed to Jake's house.

"What are you talking about? I'm not watching any house. I'm waiting to meet someone," Ivan groused.

"This is an awful isolated place to sit and wait for someone. We don't want any drug trafficking around this property. But, I don't really believe that's why you're here. I want to know why you're watching that house and who's paying you to do that?" Nick noticed Ivan start to tense and motioned for Jake to appear at the passenger window. Ivan jerked his head toward Jake when he caught a glimpse of movement.

"You're crazy, man. I'm not watching that house," Ivan said. "I'll just move to another location to call my friend to let him know." Ivan started his car.

Jake showed his gun while asking Ivan to step out of the car. Ivan had slipped the floor shift into gear while they were all talking, but neither Jake nor Nick had noticed. Ivan floored it, and away he went. Jake got the plate number, and Nick called it in. When Nick got the call back he said, "Sorry man, the plates were stolen."

A Stranger in the Will

"Naturally," Jake replied. He then proceeded to put a note on the door. He changed his office phone greeting so any potential clients would know when he'd be back. "Okay, let's stop at the hospital to see Donna, and we'll be on our way."

Nick had known Donna for years as well, so he wanted to go in also. The three of them stood by Donna's bedside giving her hugs as best they could without causing her any pain. She looked a little better this morning, but Nick, seeing her for the first time since the attack, was shocked at her appearance.

"Donna, honey, the three of us are going to Lake Tahoe for a few days to check out Julianne's house her father left her. We should be back by Monday, and the alarm will be installed then. I just wanted you to know where I would be. You can reach me on my cell phone if anything comes up. Do you know when they're letting you out?" Nick inquired.

"I heard the nurse say something about tomorrow, but I'm not sure. Jake, I'm sorry but I don't remember a lot about what he looks like. I wasn't paying attention until he started hitting me, and then my eyes closed as he raised his hand again. I just know he was a very big man."

"It's okay, don't worry about it. I think Nick and I got a good look at him this morning parked outside on the street. I'll explain later, but don't go anywhere near the office until I get back. I already took your purse and your car home to Brad early this morning. He said to tell you he'd be up after lunch. He's taking the rest of the day off."

The nurse came in to clean her wounds.

"We're going to leave now, but we'll be thinking of you." Jake said. Each of them said their goodbyes and left the hospital.

A Stranger in the Will

TWENTY

Jake and Nick had agreed to take turns driving. Jake was up first. He left the hospital parking lot and headed to Interstate 5. It would take about 7 hours, so Nick settled into the back seat for a nap while Julianne kept an eye on the road, and Jake.

"I've heard Lake Tahoe is beautiful," Julianne said. "This house must be exquisite if it's right on the water. I can't believe it's mine and that I haven't even seen it yet."

"I'll bet it's gorgeous. I'm kind of curious to see it myself." Jake smiled. They made idle chitchat as they rode along. Finally Jake had to stop, and it was a good time for Nick to take over. Julianne moved to the backseat so the guys could talk the rest of the way. She looked at Jake and realized she was happier than she should be that he was here. All that had gone on since leaving Singapore was exhausting, and it didn't take long before she fell asleep. She woke to one of them saying, "turn here!" The other replying, "no, it's farther up." She chuckled to herself.

It startled Julianne when Jake shouted. "There's the street we take down to the lake." Julianne sat upright, looking out the window. As they got down to lake level, they started checking for house numbers, mesmerized at the size and beauty of the homes.

"There, that one!" Julianne said. Nick stopped the car in the middle of the road and the three of them sat staring. Nick finally had to pull in the driveway as a car horn sounded behind them. They got out of the car and, stood, taking in the massive home in front of them. "Oh my," Julianne said. "This has to be the wrong address. What am I ever going to do with all that room?"

"Why don't we go in and see what you've inherited," Jake said. Julianne took the keys out of her purse and headed for the door. When the door swung open they couldn't move, mesmerized once more with the decor and the grandeur inside. It was more than any of them had ever experienced even with living in L.A..

"Oh Jake, this is magnificent. I wish my mother could see this."

"I believe she is watching and is very happy for you." Jake put his arm around her.

"Hey guys, come take a gander at this!" Nick shouted. Jake and Julianne hurried to where Nick was standing and looking out over Lake Tahoe.

"Wow, that is breathtaking," Julianne whispered.

"I have a great idea," Jake said. "We can order dinner in and eat out here on the deck. It would be a perfect end to a long day."

"I can't think of anything better." Julianne thought wine would top that off nicely.

Jake went to look for the liquor cabinet and was astonished at the stock on hand. He went back to Julianne and Nick. "No need to worry about ordering anything to drink. That is definitely covered."

After they finished their dinner and had a couple of glasses of wine, while enjoying the view of the lake, they decided to turn in for the night. They

A Stranger in the Will

picked up their bags on the way through the living room. Each chose a bedroom and said their goodnights.

After their doors were all closed, Jake came back out to check on doors and windows. He had a nagging feeling that something wasn't right. He checked the alarm and returned to his room.

Ivan met Jordan in a bar late that night. "I'm telling you, Ivan, this is your last chance. You have bungled three attempts already. If you don't do this, you can find yourself another job."

"I'll take care of it, they won't even know I'm there."

"I've heard that before. You better do it this time. Here are the keys and the alarm code. Get up there, and call me when it's done."

"I have to go home to get some sleep tonight. Plus, I do have a few things to finish up here before I go tomorrow, so I won't get up there until later. I'll hit them Friday night after I check everything out," Ivan assured Jordan.

"See that you do, and you will be paid handsomely. Screw up again, and you get squat." Jordan's look of steel spoke volumes.

TWENTY-ONE

The trio spent Thursday morning at breakfast, sightseeing and picking up a few groceries. The afternoon was for Jet Skiing, swimming, and a picnic lunch. That night was a nice dinner out and hitting the casinos. They were having such a good time, not thinking about all the problems back in L.A.. None of them wanted the day to end, but each made suggestions of what to do tomorrow as they headed off to bed.

Friday morning brought more of the same, with only different places to go, but definitely more time at the lake. They had planned on leaving Saturday, but took a vote for Sunday instead, as they enjoyed another dinner on the deck. A few too many glasses of wine later, they headed off to bed without a clue of what was about to happen.

Ivan arrived at Lake Tahoe in the early afternoon. His first priority was to find the house and scout it out. He found it with little difficulty and was surprised when he saw Jake and Julianne walking on the beach. Nick was on the Jet Ski. Ivan didn't see him, nor was he aware he had come up with them. Ivan took a walk around the perimeter of the house. He checked out the location of the garage and all the windows and doors. When he felt he had seen all he needed to. He stood and stared toward the beach. "Enjoy it

A Stranger in the Will

while you can," he said, as he turned and walked away.

Ivan found a hotel, had a bite to eat, gambled a little, and went for a nap. He slept longer than he'd wanted, when he woke it was pitch black in his room. It was around nine o'clock. He had planned his surprise visit for between two o'clock and three o'clock in the morning. He figured they would surely be asleep by then. After having something to eat and gambling some more, he met Lizzy and killed, the rest of his free time satisfying his own needs.

Ivan looked at the bedside clock, it was 1:15 a.m. He and Lizzy had fallen asleep after round two. It was time to take care of the business at hand, but Lizzy lying there naked, got him all revved up again. He leaned over and kissed her cheek. He meant it as a good-bye for now, but Lizzy opened her eyes. She rolled toward him and ran her hand up his inner thigh until she softly touched a sensitive spot.

"You runnin' out on me, baby?" Lizzy smiled.

"Not a chance. I have to go out for awhile. You just stay right here and rest, you'll need it for when I get back." By the time Ivan left, it was 1:45 a.m.

TWENTY-TWO

Fifteen minutes later Ivan was standing outside the enormous house. He checked the perimeter one more time to make sure all lights were out. He used the key Jordan had given him to enter the house, then, he immediately disarmed the security alarm. He only had a small penlight to use, and that didn't offer much light, but Ivan started down the hall nontheless. '*Shit!*' he thought, *way too many bedrooms*. He went through a process of elimination. The P.I. would want to put himself between her and trouble, so he would more than likely take one of the first rooms. She would be in the master, since she is, now, the lady of the house. Ivan knew where the master was by the size of the windows when he was scouting from outside. He headed to the bedroom at the end of the hall, being very careful opening the door so as not to wake his target. Julianne started to stir. Ivan backed off and waited until she settled again.

Jake hadn't been sleeping well since they arrived. He never got rid of the feeling he had the first night they were there. He still felt uneasy.

Just then, his ears perked up and, while he didn't know why, he knew himself well enough to know there was a valid reason. He quietly got out of bed, stepped into his pants, and walked over to listen at the door. Carefully he opened his door to look up and down the hall. His heart stopped as his eyes focused on Julianne's open door. He

A Stranger in the Will

backed into his room to retrieve his gun from the nightstand. He got out into the hallway and, carefully he slid down the hall with his back plastered to the wall. When he got to Julianne's room, he noticed a large figure heading toward her as she slept. He quietly stepped into the room with his gun masterly aimed. "Don't you take another step. I assure you I don't miss, even in the dark."

Ivan's vision was already accustomed to the darkness so he had no problem identifying Jake as he spun around to face him. "I'm not a bad shot myself. Are you willing to put it to a test? You get me or I get her first?"

Julianne opened her eyes. It took a minute to focus and comprehend what was happening. She asked Jake what he was doing there. Then she noticed the gun in Jake's hand and followed the direction it was pointing. Her eyes went wide when she spotted the large, masked, man all dressed in black, standing a short distance from her bed. She gasped and looked back at Jake as she started scooting to the other side of the bed.

"Look, I don't know who you are," Jake began, "but I'm pretty sure I know who sent you. Man, make sure the money is enough to make life in prison worth it".

"Julianne," Jake continued. "I want you to slide off the opposite side of the bed and walk over to me." Julianne started to do as Jake asked.

Ivan spoke up. "I don't think that's gonna happen." As Ivan was talking, Jake spotted Nick out of the corner of his right eye, sneaking down the hall.

"Man, listen to me. You can walk out of here the same way you came and in, and I won't stop you. You can go back and tell Jordan Simms we weren't here when you came and that we must have left early to go back to L.A. He'll never hear any different from us. I know that's who sent you."

"What kind of fool do you take me for? Do you have any idea what my life will be worth if I don't get this done this time?"

"You tell me how much Jordan is paying you, and Julianne will match it. If you do that, you can walk away, start a new life somewhere far away from Jordan, and never have to see him again." Jake said.

"Are you serious? You expect me to fall for that?"

"You're standing here holding a gun on her." He pointed to Julianne. What do you think?" Ivan looked toward Julianne, contemplating Jake's offer. He was thinking it sure would be nice to get out from under Simms.

"You agree to his offer of spending your money?" Ivan questioned Julianne.

"Since you're standing less than two feet away, pointing a gun at me, I'd say that's a stupid question." As Ivan was facing her, Jake was waving behind his back to Nick motioning for him to go to the living room and wait.

"Don't call me stupid!" Ivan snapped as he raised his gun.

"Okay, I'm sorry, it was a bad choice of words." Julianne apologized.

A Stranger in the Will

"Come on, man, she didn't mean anything by it. She's just scared." Jake calmly stated.

"You move over to the other side of the bed." Ivan motioned to Jake to move, pointing his gun to guide him. "Drop your gun and sit on the bed. I'll leave when I have the money. Where is it?"

Julianne told Ivan she didn't have that kind of money lying around. They'd have to wait until morning when the bank opened.

"Why don't we go out to the living room and, have something to eat while we wait. It's only a couple more hours," Jake suggested.

Ivan thought for a minute. "All right, let's go." He waved his gun toward the bedroom door. The three of them started down the hall. When they reached the living room Jake scanned the room for Nick. He didn't see him, but knew he was in the shadows.

Jake led the way to the kitchen under the pretense of raiding the refrigerator. As he opened it, he heard Nick telling Ivan to drop the gun and put his hands over his head. Jake turned around and saw Nick's gun against the nape of Ivan's neck. Jake bent over to pick up Ivan's gun and retrieve his own gun from Ivan's waistband, and the four of them went to sit in the living room.

Julianne searched the draws in the kitchen for some plastic pull ties to use as hand cuffs. She found them and took them to Jake. He bound Ivan's hands and feet. "Now," Jake said, "let's talk."

TWENTY-THREE

"I've got nothing to say," Ivan said as he looked around the room.

"What's your name?" Jake asked.

"Do you think I'm stupid enough to tell you that?"

"We'll find out anyway when the police come, you idiot," said Nick, throwing his two cents in.

Ivan looked at Nick. "Who are you anyway? I didn't see you earlier when I was here checking the place out. But I do remember you from L.A. when you two snuck up on me outside his house." He pointed to Jake.

"I'm going to be known as your worst nightmare if you don't start talking. "Nick said.

"We know you're working for Jordan Simms," Julianne chimed in. "I know he wants me out of his life, so he hired you to do his dirty work. Right?"

"Listen, maybe we can work something out if you're willing to go along with it. Otherwise, have a nice life bending over to pick up the soap," Jake said.

"You want me to make a deal with you?"

Jake shrugged his shoulders toward the others. "Okay then, your choice. Guess I'll call the police. Before you know it, we'll be back in bed for a couple more hours, but who knows what you'll be doing." Jake stood and headed toward the phone in the living room.

A Stranger in the Will

"Wait a minute, what's the deal?"

Jake sat back down. "I'm going to throw an idea out and the others have to agree with it before it's done." Julianne and Nick both nodded so Jake would continue. "If you think you can tape your conversation with Jordan, convince him that you did the job, let him pay you, and walk away, Julianne will give you an additional $25,000.00. You can move to wherever you want and start over. Hopefully in a better career. How much is Jordan paying you?"

"$50,000.00." Ivan answered.

"I will match that if you do this," Julianne said. Jake and Nick looked at her, both surprised, but they didn't say anything.

"What am I supposed to tell him if he wants proof? There won't be any police report or anything on the news to back me up. He's no fool." Ivan grimaced.

"Tell him there is no proof. You shot both of us, rented a boat, and dropped us in the deepest part of the lake. Jordan doesn't know he's here with us." Jake pointed to Nick. "We need that proof before the police will arrest a member of the Simms family."

Nick felt it was his turn to speak. "I'm warning you, if you try to double-cross us by not doing it and saying you did, or by telling Jordan about the deal and making another with him. I can guarantee that you *won't* live to regret it. Are you comprehending?"

"Yes." Ivan answered.

"Okay, what's your name?" Jake asked again.

"Ivan Slater."

"It's not that I don't trust you, Ivan Slater, but I'd like to see your license. I also want your address and phone number before you leave," Jake demanded. Ivan gave Jake all the information he wanted. Jake excused himself and went to another room and dialed Ivan's cell phone number. *Surprise, surprise*, Jake thought, that number was not in service. Jake returned to the living room and announced the deal was off. Everyone turned and stared at him.

"What's going on?" Nick asked.

"It seems this little weasel has either lied to us or not paid his cell phone bill." Jake put his hand on Ivan's shoulder and squeezed until Ivan yelled. "I went to the other room and dialed the number he gave us. Did you hear his phone ring?" Nick and Julianne both stared at Ivan while waiting for his explanation.

"All right," Julianne said. "Call the police. Even after I offered to match the money, he still lies to us? We can't trust he'll do anything we ask. I vote we find another way to get Jordan."

"No wait, I'll do it. I promise, you can even put the wire on me and sit outside Simms office," Ivan begged.

"Yeah and who's going to make sure you don't alert Jordan that you have it on?" Julianne asked, she was extremely angry. She looked at Jake. "How do we even know he won't take Jordan's money and the tape and leave town?"

"Let's try this," Jake offered. "Either Nick or I will go to Ivan's hotel with him to get his things while the other two clean up around here and get ready to go back to L.A. Ivan, give me your real

A Stranger in the Will

phone number." Jake dialed the new number Ivan gave him. "What do you know" Jake said when he dialed and it rang. "Nick, let's flip a coin to see who stays and cleans and who goes with Ivan."

"We don't have to flip a coin unless you hate to clean as much as I do." Nick said. "That's why I pay a cleaning lady."

Jake laughed. "Okay you go with Ivan. Julianne and I will be ready when you get back."

"Let me call my room first so my companion can leave before we get there." Ivan said.

"Your companion? You mean you aren't working alone?" Nick asked.

"Yes, I work alone, but I have needs just like anybody else."

"Oh, that kind of companion. Were you good enough that she'd be waiting all this time?" Nick laughed.

"Hell man, that's none of your business."

"Make your call, Casanova, so we can get going."

Nick and Ivan left after Ivan called and no one answered. As they walked out the door, Julianne couldn't hold in her laughter any longer. Jake thought how good it was to hear after all she'd been through. He only hoped it was due to humor and not a defense mechanism covering up the fear and total exhaustion that were finally catching up with her.

"Well, let's get packing," Julianne said while still giggling. Jake grabbed her hand and started down the hall. They parted at his room as she headed for hers. Jake finished packing and cleaning up his room and went to Nick's and repeated the process. All the while thinking what a wonderful setting this house would have been to have Julianne lying next to him after making love. He shook off the ache inside him and took their bags to the living room and went back down the hall to help Julianne. He knocked on her door but didn't get any response. He opened the door just enough to call out to her and he heard the shower running. That was almost his undoing. It took every bit of decency he could muster to close the door and walk away. He continued to the front of the house and started on the kitchen. By the time he finished, Julianne came out all ready to go. "I'll finish up the living room and the deck," she said. Jake nodded and turned his back to her as the vision he had when she was in the shower came rushing back. The aching he felt deep inside was showing more and more every time he looked at her.

"*Damn,*" Jake thought, *"what have I gotten myself into?"*

"Are you okay, Jake?" Julianne asked.

He turned only his head to face her. He hoped she couldn't see his slight blush. "I'm fine, just trying to get done before Ivan and Nick get back."

"What's the plan with Ivan? How are we ever going to be sure he'll get the tape we need to stop Jordan?" Julianne looked puzzled.

A Stranger in the Will

TWENTY-FOUR

Ivan and Nick came in. "All done," Nick said. He looked at Jake and knew immediately that his friend was in trouble. *Uh-oh*, he thought. Jake's cheeks were flushed, and he had that look of wanting in his eyes. Nick smiled at Jake, which embarrassed Jake even more since he knew his friend could tell.

"What's going on?" Nick said with a teasing tone and a big grin.

Jake gave him the evil eye that told him to butt out. "Just trying to figure out how we can keep old Ivan here on the straight and narrow until we have that tape in our possession." Nick's smile just grew bigger. All the while, Julianne was looking from one to the other, wondering what was going on between the two friends.

Ivan piped up. "I told you I would do it. You don't need to be fretting about my part. I want out from under Jordan Simms, and this is the only way I will ever get that. I know that now, so let's get on with it."

"Whoa, Nick what did you say to him while you were gone?" Julianne asked.

"Nothing. He's just seen the light, I guess."

"Okay, let's all sit out on the deck for a few minutes and put this together," Jake suggested. Ivan and Julianne headed outside and Nick stood next to Jake and asked him if he was sure he could sit down right now, then laughed as Jake socked him in the arm as they headed to the deck.

The view was so spectacular with the lights twinkling on the opposite shoreline. It was so breathtakingly romantic it was making Jake's personal problem urgent as hell. Knowing they had to leave, the air was filled with regret.

Julianne spoke first, breaking the silence. "Hey guys, remember, we can come back anytime we want to." She looked at Jake and Nick.

"I can't wait for that," Jake said, "but for now, let's do some brainstorming." They all threw out suggestions on how best to get Jordan Simms. Even Ivan partook in the conversation. He had some good input, but it still left Julianne skeptical and untrusting. The decision was made to put a wire on Ivan and be right outside Jordan's office, listening and taping it themselves.

Jake had all the equipment they needed. In his business they were necessary tools of the trade. Jake also had an idea to put a camera inside Jordan's office that pointed at Ivan so they would know if he tried to tip off Jordan about the wire. However, that would need to be discussed out of Ivan's earshot. Jake and Nick would take care of getting in the office to plant the camera. Jake also planned on planting a bug in case Ivan didn't do his part.

The four of them locked up and headed for the car. They drove by Ivan's hotel one more time to retrieve his car. They had some breakfast and left Lake Tahoe, for now. Except for stopping for a quick lunch about half way through the trip home,

A Stranger in the Will

everyone was pretty quiet. Nick kept Ivan company on the way back to L.A, and Jake assumed they were doing the same as he was, thinking of every possible way they could make this work. He wasn't hearing any conversation coming from Ivan's car on the walkie-talkie they had picked up, so all seemed okay so far.

TWENTY-FIVE

Ivan expected to go home to his own place before the meeting on Monday, but Jake assured him that wasn't going to happen. As they pulled into Jake's parking lot, Jake told Ivan, "you're staying with us until this is done. That way I can be sure you won't contact Jordan and set us up."

"Hey," Ivan said, "I told you I wanted to do this, too. I've had enough of Simms." Nick explained to Ivan that this was what was known as buying an insurance policy without any money changing hands.

The four of them got out of the car, stretched, and went to the trunk to get their bags.

Jake opened the door then stood back to let Julianne enter. As he looked around, the vision of Donna laying all bloodied on the floor came slamming back into his head. He spun around and got right up into Ivan's face. "If we didn't need you to do this for us, I'd kill you myself for what you did to Donna." He turned and headed up the stairs to the apartment, following Julianne.

Ivan turned hoping to head back out the door and ended up staring into the barrel of Nick's gun. Nick just smiled and waved his gun toward the stairs.

Once they were all assembled, Jake excused himself to go to his office and quickly check his messages. He was happy to find a couple of inquiries for his services. He made a note to call the potential clients in the morning. He then locked up the downstairs and again went to join the others in the apartment.

"Okay," he said, let's decide who is taking first shift tonight to make sure Ivan stays put. Nick, are you staying or going home?"

"I'll stay for tonight and tomorrow until we're done with all this on Monday. Then I'll go home."

"Thanks, buddy, I appreciate it. Julianne, I'm going to tie Ivan up here, and then Nick and I need to go downstairs to make some plans. Are you going to be all right here with Ivan by yourself for a few minutes?"

"I'm sure I'll be fine."

"You don't need to do that," Ivan huffed.

"Oh, I think I do, Ivan, and if you try anything, you won't need to worry about your meeting with Jordan. We'll be right downstairs, just yell if you need us." Jake rubbed Julianne's arm and soon realized he shouldn't have touched her.

He and Nick turned and walked down to the office. Jake started to explain to his friend what his idea was for a camera and bug in Jordan's office so it would show if Ivan pointed to the wire.

"Good idea. You and I can take a run over there, it won't take long. I can call a buddy of mine to come and sit with Julianne and Ivan until we get back." Nick said.

"Call him, the sooner we get this done, the better," Jake yelled back as he headed upstairs to tell Julianne what was going on. Nick came up a few minutes later and told Jake his friend would be there in about a half an hour. Jake took Julianne in the bedroom to explain that Nick's friend was coming over to sit with her and what he and Nick were headed out to do.

"Are you sure you're going to be able to get into Jordan's office to plant those things? He must have the best security money can buy," Julianne whispered.

"I have no doubt about that, but I have the equipment to see them in the dark and we can safely Taser them if need be." Julianne looked puzzled and worried for the safety of the two friends she had made. "It'll be fine, I promise," Jake said as he drew her into his embrace to comfort her. His arms around her felt so good and reassuring that, she didn't want him to let go. Jake knew he better stand back, or else this mission tonight would never take place. As he released her she felt a bit empty inside. They both stood there staring into each other's eyes, but their trance was broken by the sound of the doorbell downstairs. Their sitter had arrived. *Excellent timing*, Jake thought, while Julianne wished she could stay safe in his arms.

A Stranger in the Will

TWENTY-SIX

Jake and Nick loaded all the necessary equipment into Jake's truck. Julianne was watching out the window, thinking they looked like a synchronized team already, while loading up. She knew they would be a force to be reckoned with as they performed their tasks. Still, she would worry until they came home.

As the truck pulled into a field across and down the street from Simms Trading, the two men put on their night equipment, putting the camera and bug in Jake's backpack. Their stun guns and tranquilizer guns secured at their sides, they were ready to approach the compound. Crouched along the fence line, they took notice of guards and their scheduled walks. Jake tested the fence to see if it was electric, it wasn't. They couldn't scale over the top either, it had razor wire curling over it. He removed cutting tools from Nick's backpack and began to work on a section of the fence. They crawled on their stomachs through the hole they had made, and still crouching, continued on toward the building.

Ivan had given them the location of Jordan's office before they left. They hoped they were headed in the right direction. While avoiding yard lights and guards, they got to where they thought Ivan said the office was. Jake motioned to his friend to look up at the window where a light was shinning. Their adrenaline was pumping at the possibility of Jordan still being there. Jake, being the larger and stronger of the two, held Nick on his shoulders while he peered through the window. He didn't see anyone and thought the lamp simply served as a night-light. While up there, Nick tried to assess the alarm system on the window. He couldn't see very well, just enough of the alarm stuck out to know where it was located, but not what kind it was. They both knew the time was coming for a guard to do his security check, so they had to move. Nick got off Jake's shoulders, and they whispered to each other their ideas about disarming the alarm. Just as they were ready to put Nick back on Jake's shoulders, a guard was coming around the corner. He was still far enough away that he wouldn't be able to see them in their dark clothing. They both flattened themselves against the building, waiting for the guard to come closer. The guard fell to the ground as the Taser hit, and they dragged him behind a couple of decorative plants and continued with their plan.

Nick and Jake spotted the wires on the outside of the building at the roofline. Nick threw a grappling hook to the rooftop and climbed the rope to disconnect the wires for the alarm system. Back down the rope and onto Jake's shoulders, he proceeded to use a sharp instrument to jimmy the window lock. He climbed in, pulling Jake in behind him. They placed the camera in a planter behind Jordan's desk, facing the guest seats and the bug went under Jordan's chair.

A Stranger in the Will

When the doorknob turned, they scrambled to hide behind the massive desk, but it was only the guard checking to make sure the door was locked. After packing up their supplies they crawled back out the window. Jake went first so Nick could land on his shoulders. As Nick slid out he reengaged Jordan's window lock. He grabbed the rope still hanging by his side and climbed back up to the roof to remove the clip so the alarm system would reset.

As they headed back to the fence, they brushed their footprints away and soldered the fence so it would take a scrutinizing look to tell it had been cut.

As Jake pulled into his parking lot, Julianne stopped pacing and ran to the window. The two men came in, locked up, and went upstairs. Julianne opened the apartment door and threw herself into Jake's arms.

"My God, I was a mess, it was taking so long. I thought you had been caught. I was so scared thinking of what Jordan would do."

"It all went very well," Jake said as he kissed her on top of the head. He looked at Ivan and told him they would see every move he made while there, so it would be in his best interest to stick to the plan.

"I will," Ivan said.

"Okay, let's set up our babysitting schedule for the night." Julianne chose to go first since the men had already put in a full nights work. "Are you sure?" Jake asked. Nick's friend had already left, so it was just the three of them to cover the night.

"I'm sure. It's ten o'clock now, so I cover until one o'clock, then one of you until four o'clock and the other until seven. That schedule will give each of us only three hours." Jake and Nick chose their shifts and headed off to bed. Ivan just rolled his eyes.

The next morning Julianne had breakfast going while the guys had Ivan make his call to Jordan. The appointment was set for two o'clock. Jake reminded Ivan that he would walk away from L.A. with a lot of money if he pulled this off, but Jake didn't have to remind him. Ivan was anxious to get it over with and be on his way to a new life without Jordan or the three of them in it.

A Stranger in the Will

TWENTY-SEVEN

Nick and Jake spent their time planning how to remove their equipment when the job was done. They decided since Jordan didn't know Nick, he would be the one to go in the building and raise a fuss with security at the entrance. He would insist on seeing Jordan about Julianne, which would ensure Jordan's curiosity and his desire to leave his office to see what it was about. Then, Jake would sneak in and remove the camera and bug while Jordan was downstairs talking to Nick.

Lunchtime came and went, but no one was hungry, it was time to go. Ivan was very nervous, and the rest of them were very skeptical that this would go off smoothly. Jake went over some of the details again. Ivan, beginning to get annoyed at their constant badgering, shot back at them to shut the hell up.

"I know Jordan better than you do. He'll be very happy when I tell him it's over. I'll collect my money and get shooed out of there. He's not one for conversation with people who are beneath him, so he won't be into idle chitchat."

"Okay, I apologize for our skepticism," Jake said. "But you tried to kill us, Ivan. That tends to make people not trust you. You do realize that?"

"I know, but it was nothing personal, I was just doing a job. I'm glad I didn't get away with it. I kinda like you guys. I really appreciate what you're doing for me."

"Let's go and get this done. We'll meet you back at the parking place down the road. If you convince Jordan we're dead, you'll get your money and we'll never see you again, right?"

"Exactly right," Ivan said.

"All right, here we go." Jake headed for the door. Julianne stopped him to wish them all luck. She leaned forward and kissed Jake and pleaded that they both come back safely. Nick got a peck on the cheek, and Ivan wanted to know where his share was. Jake immediately pushed him out the door. They arrived at the prearranged meeting spot as Ivan drove past them to Simms Trading. Jake set up the monitor and speaker and settled in with Nick to listen and watch. As they heard Ivan enter Jordan's office, they did their adjustments to make sure everything was as clear as possible.

They watched Ivan sit in one of the fancy chairs in front of Jordan's massive mahogany desk.

"Well, Ivan, is it done?" Jordan asked.

"Yep, the alarm and key worked fine, and I caught them off guard while they slept."

"What do you mean them, and where's my proof?" Jordan asked.

"All three of them. Julianne, the P.I. she hired and their friend. Don't know who he was. I don't have any proof, just my word. I rented a boat, took them out to the middle of the lake, and made a midnight dump in the deepest part," Ivan answered.

"And I'm suppose to just take your word for that?" Jordan was suspicious. "What happens when they surface?" Ivan explained what he heard about people being dumped in that lake, they never surface.

"Mr. Simms, I'm not stupid enough to lie to you. I know you'd send someone else after me." Ivan was starting to fidget and sweat. Jordan sat and sized him up for a few minutes. Jake and Nick were holding their breath as they sat in the van, watching.

"Okay, Ivan, here you are $50,000.00. I hope you know there is no where you can hide if I find you didn't kill Julianne Sullivan."

"Believe me, I know, and thank you," Ivan said as he lifted the money to the air.

"All right, just get out of here, and you'll hear from me if I need you again," Jordan stated.

On that note, Ivan got up and hightailed it out of the office, whispering to himself,"I don't think so," as he smiled all the way out of the building. He hurried back to where Jake and Nick were waiting.

"Good job, Ivan. Now if I were you, I'd get back to your apartment and take just what is absolutely important to you and get out of town fast." Jake handed him the $50,000.00 Julianne had promised him. "Try to put together a better life for yourself, no matter where you end up."

"Believe me, I will. I'm getting to old for this kind of work. I need some rest," Ivan laughed. He shook hands with his two partners in this scam and left.

TWENTY-EIGHT

"Well, I guess we're up," Nick said as he got in the driver's seat and headed up the road. He pulled into a parking spot where it would be difficult for anyone to see Jake exit the vehicle as well. Nick entered the building through the main entrance, as Jake entered through a maintenance door.

Nick approached the security desk and advised the guard that he needed to speak with Jordan Simms. When the guard asked who he was and what it was regarding, Nick said his name was Stanley Knowles and it was regarding a Ms. Julianne Sullivan. Nick watched as the guard dialed Jordan's number and listened as he said, "Mr. Simms, I have a gentleman here at the desk, says his name is Stanley Knowles. He needs to speak to you about a Julianne Sullivan."

Jordan immediately felt nausea creep into his stomach. His head started spinning wondering what Ivan had done. "Mr. Simms, do you want me to send him up?" The guard interrupted Jordan's train of thought.

"Yes, I'm sorry, please bring him up." Jordan said as he tried to regain his composure. The guard told one of the escorts to take Mr. Knowles to Mr. Simms's office.

"Nick said, "Oh, excuse me, I'm not going up there. I want him to come down here where we will be around other people so I don't end up dead." The guard looked at him, wondering if he

A Stranger in the Will

was for real. The guard tried to convince him to go up to Jordan's office, but he finally had to call Jordan again. The guard explained that Mr. Knowles wouldn't come up, he wanted him to come down to talk where there were other people around.

"What?" Jordan said. "What are you talking about?"

"He won't come up, Mr. Simms. Says if you want to know what he has to say you have to come down here."

"All right, I'll be down in a minute. Search him first, and make sure he's not concealing any weapons. He sounds like a kook."

Jordan was very nervous, and that wasn't a common emotion for him. As he exited the elevator he looked around, and the guard pointed to Nick sitting on a bench. Jordan walked over to him and introduced himself.

Meanwhile, Jake was entering Jordan's office. He pulled the camera down, removed the bug from under Jordan's chair, then left the building the same way he entered. When he reached the truck a vibration went off in Nick's pocket to alert him that Jake's part was done and he was safely back at the truck. Now Nick had to get out of his predicament.

"What can I do for you Mr. Knowles?"

"I understand you need a Julianne Sullivan taken care of, if you know what I mean?" Nick said.

"Where did you hear such a thing?" Jordan tried hard to remain calm while listening to the stranger's explanation.

"I heard some guy talking about it in a bar a few nights ago. He mentioned your name. It took me a few days to get the nerve to ask you, but if you really needed someone to do that for you. I'd take on the job for a reasonable fee."

"Well, I'm sorry you wasted your time, Mr. Knowles, but I'm not in the business of hiring hitmen. If you see that person again, I hope you tell him he is misinformed. You have a nice day." Jordan turned and walked away, relieved that it was nothing earth shattering.

Nick walked out of sight of the guard and ran the rest of the way to the truck. He hopped in, and they took off back to Jake's office, feeling as though they had put an end to that. Now Jake just had to get the police to listen to him and the tape.

The two of them laughed all the way back to Jake's. They weren't sure if it was attributed to adrenaline or pride in a job well done.

For the second time Julianne had paced the whole time they were gone. She heard the truck pull up and ran downstairs, shut off the alarm, and opened the door. She saw Jake standing there with open arms and a smile. She ran to him. He picked her up and twirled her around, and, at that moment, she knew they were successful. When Jake put her down, her beautiful green eyes locked with his sexy blues for what seemed like forever. Nick just stood back and watched, happy that his friend found someone he really cared about, even if Jake didn't know how much yet.

Finally Nick said, "Oh my God you guys, get a room." Julianne looked at Nick and burst out

A Stranger in the Will

laughing. They all turned and went inside. Nick gathered up his things and, shook hands with his friend as they agreed it all worked out very well. Julianne gave him another kiss on the cheek and thanked him for all his help. Nick started his car and drove away, anxious to get home to his own surroundings.

Jake locked up, and they both went upstairs. They said goodnight as they headed for their separate bedrooms. Neither one was sure that the occasional kisses meant anything more than Julianne's gratitude or Jake's compassion for her circumstances.

The next day, Jake felt Ivan had enough time to get out of dodge, so to speak. Now it was time for Julianne to call Christopher Romano with her decision to stay and learn the business at Simms Trading.

Julianne made the call to inform the attorney. Romano told her he would relay her decision to Madeline Simms right away, and that she would be hearing from one of them as to when and where to report and get started. She thanked him and hung up. Now the wait began. The ball would be in Jordan's court once again.

Jake and Julianne both hoped Ivan had already left, or he'd be a dead man for sure.

TWENTY-NINE

That night, unaware of what Jordan had paid Ivan to do, Madeline broke the news to her son of Julianne's decision.

Jordan told his mother that Romano made a mistake. Julianne must have told him days ago and he was just getting around to telling them now.

"Jordan, he said she just called him this morning." Jordan spun around. He was losing control, his head was spinning and, his anger was growing. Kylie just sat there, watching her brother's rapid meltdown.

"Jordan, what's the matter with you?" Madeline asked as she looked at Kylie for answers. Kylie truly wasn't aware of how far Jordan had gone, but she knew it wasn't good.

Again his mother tried to break him out of his frenzy. Realizing he was way too upset over the news, she yelled, "Oh my God Jordan, what have you done?"

Jordan turned and looked at his mother. His jaw was set, and his eyes looked deep and frightening. "Never mind, Mother, you don't want to know." He left the room as his mother continued to call after him. He pulled his cell phone out and dialed Ivan's phone. No answer, but still connected.

Jordan then placed a call to an acquaintance named Joe, hoping he could get him someone else to take care of Julianne Sullivan, as well as Ivan

A Stranger in the Will

Slater. *I warned you what would happen if you crossed me, Ivan,* he thought to himself.

Joe didn't return the call until the next morning. He assured Jordan he had the perfect person. He gave him Blake's name, but didn't elaborate on skills. Joe didn't want to spoil the surprise of his choice.

Jordan was sitting behind his desk shuffling papers, trying to concentrate on business matters that needed his attention, but all he kept looking at was his cell phone sitting on his desk and not ringing. Annoyed that Blake hadn't called yet, he went to his office liquor cabinet and poured himself a stiff drink. For every drink he poured, his mind went to darker and more evil ways to get even with Ivan for betraying him.

Finally his phone rang, and he sprinted across his large office and grabbed it as it danced in place on his desk. "Hello, Simms here."

"Mr. Simms, this is Blake Masters. Joe said you have a job of some urgency?" Jordan just stood there, he couldn't believe the voice he was listening to.

"Mr. Simms, are you there?"

"Yes I am, but I think there has been some mistake. I'm not sure you can handle what I need done. I don't understand what Joe was thinking. I'm sorry, Blake, I will take this up with Joe. Thank you for calling." As Jordan hung up, he looked up to see a beautiful woman walk into his office unannounced. "Excuse me, you can't just walk in here. This is a private office. How did you get this far, anyway?"

"Because I'm that good, Mr. Simms. I often do this to prove a point, and I so enjoy the shock factor I'm getting from you right now."

"You're Blake?"

"The one and only, sir."

"Well, I must say, I'm very impressed. Please have a seat, Ms. Masters. You certainly proved you're capable of sneaking up on people, but this assignment will require much more than your obvious skills at being stealthy. There will be surveillance, hunting your prey, and eliminating them."

"Mr. Simms, why do think it took me so long to call you, and how do you think I knew where your office was located in this massive building? It's called surveillance. I also carry a gun, and in the time it took you to notice me standing inside your office, you would have been dead without ever knowing what hit you."

Jordan's mouth curled up slightly as he tried not to show his amusement. She was good, no doubt, and cocky as hell. He liked her though and was actually thinking of giving her a shot. He didn't know if it was because she was proving herself to be a formidable opponent or because he found her cockiness very sexy and was imagining what it would be like between the sheets when this was over.

"Okay, are you on any other assignments right now? This will call for your undivided attention and absolute secrecy. No talking to friends or family or even Joe about what you have to do." He searched her face for a sign that she could or could not abide by that. He saw nothing.

A Stranger in the Will

"It's kind of late, so be back here tomorrow morning at nine o'clock. That will give me time to draft instructions and gather pictures."

"You bet. See you then." By the time Jordan got out of his chair, buttoned his suit jacket, and started walking around his desk to shake her hand, his door was closing, yet he never even heard her get up from her chair. He just stood there wondering how she did that, knowing her stealth would be a great asset.

The next morning Blake showed up at nine o'clock sharp. She decided to announce herself to guard in the lobby. Jordan needed to know she could abide by the rules as well.

Jordan had stayed late last night and come in early this morning, his adrenaline surging. He had a great plan put together, and he knew it would work smoothly as long as Blake followed it. *Blake being female is going to be my ace in the whole. Her prey will never suspect*, he thought to himself.

His phone rang, and the guard at the front entrance announced that Ms. Masters was waiting to see him. "By all means, send her up, " Jordan said with anticipation in his tone and a smile on his face.

"Good morning Mr. Simms," Blake said as she entered Jordan's office. "I hope you were able to put together all the information I need to start this job. I'm anxious to get on it."

"I believe I have everything in place, Blake, and please call me Jordan." Blake nodded her head in agreement as they set out to discuss and finalize the scenario that would eliminate the two thorns in Jordan's side.

"I want you to locate Ivan Slater first. He handed her a picture of Ivan and explained how he had double-crossed him. 'Here is his last address and cell phone number. I don't think I need to tell you where to start or how to do your job. I hope you don't prove me wrong. I've never worked with a female on these matters."

"That's probably why you need one now." Blake smiled at him. Jordan smiled back, impressed with her confidence.

She flipped through the plan he had made and studied the pictures of her targets, as well as Jake Matthews.

"You want the P.I. done too?"

"Yes, he'll only become a problem after the girl is gone. He'll want revenge. I'm suppose to call Julianne and arrange a meet with her to start working here. I think it'll be better to let her start and work for awhile before anything happens to her. It won't seem so suspicious if I befriend her and start training her. I assure you it won't be easy, but I think I can convince her that I had a change of heart. So, what are your thoughts?"

"I don't think you have anything to worry about. I'll keep you advised of my progress in regards to Ivan and then meet with you again before I take care of the P.I."

"Sounds great." Jordan pushed a manila envelope across his desk that contained her down payment for services and expenses. Blake rose from her chair, sent a cocky salute to Jordan, and left.

A Stranger in the Will

Kylie knocked on his door and entered. "Well, how goes the battle with Ms. Hot pants? Jordan smiled at his sister's remark. "Is she taking the assignment?"

"Yes she is. She's going for Ivan first. Julianne will start here tomorrow, and we'll give her some time so we won't be under suspicion when the time comes."

"I guess I'm not as convinced as you that she can handle this. Are you sure you're thinking from your brain and not from somewhere else?"

"Yes, I'm sure. Now get out of here, I have work to do." Jordan secretly was concerned that maybe he wasn't thinking from the right body part.

THIRTY

On Blake's way home she stopped by the address Jordan had given her for Ivan's apartment. She watched the building for awhile to see if he went in or out. She really didn't expect he was still around but wanted to be a tad more confident in that thought before she went to question the manager. She walked up to the mailboxes and checked the one with Ivan's name on it. Empty. She rang the bell for his unit, but heard nothing. Just then an elderly couple approached the steps.

"Can we help you? We're James and Susan Olsen. We manage this building."

"I was just going to ring your bell. My name is Joanne Slater, and I was looking for my cousin, Ivan," Blake said.

"Oh, I'm sorry dear, Ivan moved out suddenly a few days ago. He was on a month-to-month, and he chose not to stay."

"I really need to find him. You wouldn't know where he went by any chance? Is he having you forward his mail or his deposit refund?"

"No, I'm so sorry, but we gave him his refund after we inspected the apartment the day he left. He must be having the post office tend to his mail."

"Okay, thank you anyway," Blake said as she turned and walked away. Now that she knew the element of surprise was not going to work, she dialed his cell phone.

A Stranger in the Will

Ivan was hesitant to answer, the number didn't look familiar, but he picked up anyway. "Hello."

"Ivan, this is Sandra Olsen. I am James Olsen's niece." There was silence. "Ivan, I do the bookkeeping for my uncle on the apartments. When they paid you your deposit refund they shorted you the interest it had earned as well as the return of your cleaning deposit. Thank you for leaving the unit in such good condition. It totals $300.00 and I need to know where you would like the check sent."

Ivan had chosen to stay in a small motel off the strip in Lake Tahoe. He knew that, if Jordan was looking for him, he didn't want to be obviously spending the money he had left L.A. with.

"James and Susan never mentioned anything about a cleaning deposit or interest. I don't remember ever paying a cleaning deposit."

"You did, and you can feel free to call James and verify it with him if you wish." Blake was making a face hoping she was convincing Ivan she was on the up and up. She obviously didn't want him checking with his landlords.

"Yeah, I will have to do that first. This doesn't sound right. Give me your number, and I'll call you back." Blake hung up, and Ivan knew then it was a setup. Jordan had found out what he had done. He knew he would have to get as far away as possible, quicker than he had planned. He wondered if the woman who called had traced the call to the motel. He wasn't taking any chances. He packed his bag, paid the bill and drove into California. That night he stayed at a hotel near the San Francisco airport. He would decide from there where he wanted to go. Flights were plentiful anywhere out of San Francisco.

Blake was checking her system at home, trying to trace the call to Ivan. *Gotcha*, she said to herself. *Not too smart, Mr. Slater, Lake Tahoe isn't nearly far enough to escape.* She got busy on her computer tracking down which hotel Ivan was staying at. She found where he had been registered, but he had checked out shortly after her call. *Shit, where did you go, Ivan?*

As Ivan laid on his bed trying to piece together a life somewhere unfamiliar to him, he wondered if he had done the right thing. He could be home in the life that was comfortable for him. *Oh well*, he thought, *too late now*. He continued to look at the map laid out in front of him, his eyes scanning exotic places his mind couldn't comprehend. *That's it*, he said to himself. *I am not letting Jordan Simms chase me out of my own country.* He turned the light out as his mind settled on going back to the L.A. area. *It's a big city, I'm sure I can stay out of Jordan's sights, he said.*

A Stranger in the Will

THIRTY-ONE

Meanwhile, Julianne was getting ready to start her new job at Simms Trading tomorrow morning.

Christopher Romano had given Jordan her cell phone number, and they had made the necessary arrangements for Julianne to start her training. "I don't get it, " Julianne said to Jake as they were having dinner. "One minute he wants to kill me, and the next he's all nice and wanting me to get started with training. What do you think he's up to? I know it has to be a ruse. People just don't do an about-face like that without something attached. It's a little scary."

"Julianne, I have been asking myself that question since you talked to him earlier. I didn't want to bring it up so it was uppermost in your mind. I didn't realize you thought it, too. You're going to have to be very careful while there. You make sure you are never alone with him. If you're in his office, make sure the door remains open. I don't like this one bit, and I wish you would reconsider getting involved with the business. You have plenty of money to start a new life. You don't need this job."

"I look at it this way, Jake. If he does plan to do me any harm, at least we can bring him out in the open and get this over with and see him behind bars. Then it'll be over. I won't have to hide from him anymore."

"Yeah, if you survive whatever it is he'll try to do. Julianne, I have grown very fond of you, and I don't like the thought of you not being around here every day. Not to mention I can't protect you while you're at Simms Trading all day. I honestly don't know what I would do if he hurt you. Besides, who's going to do my clerical stuff?" Jake laughed, but the situation was far from funny. He was scared to his bones for Julianne. She was taking an awful risk.

"Oh come on, Jake, let's not be so morbid. We're having a wonderful dinner, and it's a beautiful night out here on the terrace. Let's not spoil it by speculating what might be. Besides, Donna will be back Monday, and all will be back to normal. If this works out and Jordan is on the up and up, I'll be able to move on to a place of my own and give you your space back."

That very instant Jake felt a shot right through his heart at the thought of Julianne moving out. He stood up and walked to her side of the table, took her hand, and helped her rise from her seat. "You didn't understand what I meant when I said I was very fond of you?" Their eyes locked, and Julianne blushed as she understood exactly what he meant. Jake took her into his arms. Julianne tilted her head to accept the kiss she had wanted for a long time. It was breathtaking, soft, and passionate. They both felt it and knew what was happening between them.

Julianne broke away and stared into Jake's handsome face. "I've been giving it a lot of thought, and I think I want to take it from here with Jordan by myself. I don't want you in the

A Stranger in the Will

middle anymore where you or Donna could be hurt again. I would never forgive myself if anything happened to either of you. It was hard enough for me not to pack up and go back to Singapore after Ivan attacked Donna. I couldn't handle it if he"... Jake forced her silence by putting a finger over her soft lips.

"There is no way in hell I'm going to stand back and let you deal with Jordan alone. Julianne, you have to know by now how dangerous he is and how determined he is to keep you out of Simms Trading and his life. This training thing is nothing more than a smoke screen to lure you in. You're more than a client now, and I don't want you to move out. Judging from that kiss, I'm guessing you feel something for me as well."

"I do, Jake, that's exactly why I don't want you involved with Jordan or his goons anymore. If he still wants me out of the way, he'll get rid of you first, so you can't stop him. Then he'll get me anyway. There's no sense in both of us being in harm's way."

"This is not open for anymore discussion. I'm absolutely not going to stand back and let Jordan play his games. Starting now, I'm off your payroll. This is personal." Jake started clearing off the table and returned to the kitchen. Julianne joined him in the cleanup. As she entered the kitchen she noticed Jake's profile as he faced the sink. His jaw was set and his face was red. He was angry with her, and she knew she had hurt him. She approached him and placed her hands on his shoulders and leaned into his back. "Jake, I'm so sorry. I would never intentionally hurt you. I was just trying to keep you safe. This is my first experience with having my life threatened. I'm not really sure how to handle it."

"I'm not trying to control your life, Julianne. I'm just worried to let you go there tomorrow. He's a psycho, and I know he has a plan. I can feel it."

"Okay, is there something I can do so you can have a little input as to what's going on tomorrow? A wire or something that you can listen in on?"

"If you would be willing to do that, I can arrange something. While I would still prefer you not go at all, that would be second best. I'll go downstairs and put something together." He turned and took Julianne in his arms for a bear hug. "Thank you," he whispered in her ear.

After some heavy discussion that evening, they decided it was time to turn in so Julianne would be at the top of her game tomorrow. Jake gave her a good night kiss that rocked her senses, then locked up and headed for his bedroom. Julianne headed for hers, showered, put on her nightgown, and turned down her bedcovers. As she sat on the edge of the bed, a million thoughts were flying through her head, one being that she didn't want to sleep alone tonight. Even if she didn't admit it to Jake, she was scared, and wondered if she was pushing Jordan to the brink of disaster, for her. She stood and put her robe on and headed down the hall to Jake's room.

She knocked on his door. When it opened, the sight of Jake caught her breath, he was standing here with only his pajama bottoms on, and she was looking at his bare chest. She had never seen him without a shirt before. He had a strong, masculine body.

"What is it Julianne? Are you okay?"

She shook her head to shake herself out of her trance. "Yes, I'm fine. Well, maybe I'm not. I don't want to tell you I'm scared. I don't want you talking me out of going, but I am very much afraid of Jordan."

"Oh baby, come here." He opened his arms, and she fell right into them and felt safer than she ever had in her life. "You know how I feel about you going, but it's not up to me to make that decision."

"I know, and I appreciate you not pushing me. I know how you feel, Jake, but even being afraid, I have to do this. Can I stay with you tonight and you just hold me for awhile? Maybe some of your strength will transfer to me." She smiled up at him, knowing how silly that sounded.

"Come on," Jake said as he escorted her to his bed. He pulled the blanket and sheet down on the unused side of his bed where he, more often than not, slept alone. Julianne took off her robe and climbed in.

Jake knew this was going to be the ultimate test of his chivalry. He wondered if he could really do this, his male need already pounding. He turned out the light as he joined her. He stretched his arm over and pulled her to him. Julianne couldn't believe he agreed to do this, but she was grateful he did. They both fell off to sleep in the comfort of each other's arms.

THIRTY-TWO

Jake woke with Julianne curled against his back, and she felt so good. He turned to face her. Looking at her, he couldn't believe how he made it all night without making love to this incredibly gorgeous woman lying next to him. He gave her a soft kiss on her forehead to gently wake her before his previous thoughts took over.

"Good morning. It's time to start your new adventure. I'm going to the kitchen to make us some breakfast, come on out when you're ready."

"Okay, that sounds wonderful," Julianne said as she blushed. She was a little embarrassed waking up in his bed. She waited until Jake headed into his bathroom before she slipped out of bed and went to her own room.

After breakfast Jake set her up with a wire and drove her to Simms Trading. Julianne was hesitant to get out of the car. She looked at Jake, pleading with her eyes for some reassurance from him. He didn't let her down, his smile lifted her heart. He kissed her hand, wished her luck, and reminded her he would be with her all day as he listened to everything being said. Julianne leaned across the seat and kissed him on the lips, silently saying thank you. Jake winked at her, and she felt she would melt as she opened the car door and got out.

He watched her walk through the doors while every nerve in his body was on high alert.

A Stranger in the Will

Julianne introduced herself to the guard at the desk and explained why she was there. He shook her hand and welcomed her to Simms Trading. "It'll be just a minute, if you want to have a seat. I'll call Mr. Simms and let him know you're waiting."

"Thank you, "Julianne said as she walked toward the exquisite waiting area. She twiddled her thumbs and crossed and uncrossed her legs numerous times. Just as she thought maybe she should just sneak out and forget the whole thing, the guard walked up and told her that Mr. Simms was ready for her. The guard escorted Julianne to Jordan's office. When they entered, Jordan thanked the guard and asked him to shut the door on the way out. Julianne spoke up and told Jordan she would prefer the door remain open. Jordan nodded his head to the guard, and the door was left open.

Jake smiled to himself as he listened, thrilled that Julianne had said that.

Jordan smiled at Julianne and motioned for her to have a seat in one of the leather chairs facing his desk. The atmosphere in the room was tense. Jordan knew she was nervous, and he was enjoying every minute. But her attention was actually on Jake and Nick, as she pictured them planting the surveillance equipment in this office the night they broke in. That reminded her that Jake was listening.

Jordan broke her out of her trance as he began to speak. "I must apologize for my behavior in Christopher Romano's office. I was not expecting to see you there, let alone to find out you were entitled to an inheritance from my father. I'm afraid we got off on the wrong foot. I needed time to absorb what happened that day."

Jake did not believe the BS that was coming out of Jordan's mouth as he listened in. Neither did Julianne, but they had both already agreed not to mention Ivan. But oh, how she wanted to!

Kylie walked into the office, said hello to Julianne, and sat in the chair next to her. Jordan introduced Kylie just in case Julianne didn't remember her from the day of the reading of the will. She assured them she did.

"Okay, let's get started," Jordan said. "Julianne, you will be training with Kylie first. She's our office manager, and we felt that would be the best place for you to start. It's a very important part of the whole operation. You will probably spend a month or so with management in each department so you will be introduced to the whole operation. Management meetings will be required regardless of the time of day. I'll be making up a schedule for you to follow as far as the order of departments you will be training in. It will also have your hours, lunch, and break times. At the end of today Kylie will provide you with a booklet containing rules, dress codes, regulations, vacation, and insurance options. I think that's about it for now. I wish you luck, and I hope you are as excited about a career here as we are to have you." Jordan extended his hand to Julianne as he welcomed her to Simms Trading. Jake just shook his head, what a bunch of crap.

A Stranger in the Will

Kylie and Julianne stood. Julianne thanked Jordan as she headed for the door. Kylie turned and smiled at her brother as an understanding passed between them.

The two women entered the finance department. As they shut the door to Kylie's office, Julianne was impressed by the lavish decor. Kylie knew she could make Julianne's day a living hell, but something inside her made her feel she wanted to give her a chance. The conversation they were having as they walked to her office made Kylie feel different about Julianne, even though she didn't know why.

The day came to an end, and Julianne was exhausted. Kylie had put her to the test, but she had handled it very well. It was Kylie's turn to be impressed. Julianne left the office knowing she had pulled her weight today and proved herself capable.

Jake was waiting in the prearranged parking spot that was far enough away from the doors that no one would see him. He spotted Julianne walking toward him with a certain confidence in her stride. His heart fluttered at the site of her. "She is a beauty, he said out loud. Julianne opened the car door and slid into the passenger's seat.

THIRTY-THREE

Jake started the car and drove away from Simms Trading. "Well, how did it go? I didn't hear anything that caused the hair on the back of my neck to go up, but I heard a lot of crap from Jordan."

"I thought it went pretty well, actually. Kylie wasn't anywhere near as threatening as I thought she would be. A few times I got the impression she was trying to be, but couldn't quite pull it off. It's only been one day, but I liked her."

"You still need to be careful. Kylie may not be mean by nature, but she could still be a puppet for Jordan, and he's controlling the strings."

"I guess, but I'm usually a good judge of character. After all, I thought you were very sweet when I first met you." She waited for a reaction to the sweet part, trying not to laugh.

Jake pulled into his driveway, walked around and opened Julianne's door and stared at her until he couldn't hold it in any longer. "Sweet, is that what you think? I'm a private investigator, I'm supposed to be tough, not sweet." He noticed the twinkle in her beautiful green eyes as she looked at him sheepishly. She burst out laughing.

As they entered the living room she said, "Okay, so I thought you looked very strong and capable of doing your job." Again, he looked at her, wanting better than that. "What?" she said. Jake cocked his head and had that begging look in his

A Stranger in the Will

eyes, wanting her to say it. There was that twinkle again as she made him wait. "Okay, and quite sexy, I might add. "She wrapped her arms around his neck. Just as he bent to kiss her, she said, "I'm hungry. Let's have some dinner." She broke away with a huge grin on her face.

Jake knew she was teasing, and he had plans for the payback later. He would make the kind of love to her she would never forget. He turned to follow her into the kitchen when a shot rang out in his living room. Jake grabbed her, and they both tumbled to the floor as glass from his picture window shattered around them. "Stay down!" he said, as he ran for his gun.

Blake had decided that, since Ivan was in the wind right now, she would take care of Jake and Julianne. She saw them in an embrace near the window. *Stay right there*, she said to herself, as she aimed her rifle and pulled the trigger. She held her position, waiting to see if anyone peered out the window to look around. Suddenly Jake burst through the back door. He was crouched down, sweeping the area with his gun. He stood and walked toward the bushes in the back of the property, using the trajectory of the bullet to guide him to the shooter's position. As he examined the area it was obvious someone had been there. The grass was pressed to the earth, and there were footprints in the dirt. *Small footprints*, he thought, *a woman or a very small man*. He followed the prints as far as they were available, and heard a vehicle peeling out in the distance. He knew he wouldn't make it in time, so he headed back to Julianne.

"Are you okay, honey?"

"Just a little rattled, but otherwise I'm okay." Jake helped her up and took her into a bear hug. He was shaking himself as he tried to help her stop.

"Julianne," he said, "you can't go back there tomorrow. I'm going to call Nick to stay with you while I go have a talk with Jordan. That was too close."

"Jake, he won't admit anything. It's useless to go and dangerous to confront him alone. I agree that this job is over until things are under control. Maybe Kylie would be willing to help us, although I doubt it just yet. But right now I think we should call the police and get this documented for when we have more evidence to go with it."

While waiting for the police to come, they made a couple of sandwiches that would be dinner for tonight. Jake's plans for Julianne tonight would have to wait. His first priority was to keep her safe, and that meant staying alert. While they were eating he decided to tell her he had gone to the police station with the tape from Ivan.

"What did they say? Why didn't you tell me you were going?"

"I didn't want you distracted while there today. I figured I could tell you tonight. It wasn't real positive anyway. They said they would check it out, but they didn't seem in too much of a hurry. After all the trouble we went through to get it, I'm not sure it will help us. They so much as insinuated it could be a fake. They were more concerned with how I got it than what was on it. We may still need more." Julianne sat there, trying to understand, until the police showed up.

After filling out the police report and talking to the officer who responded, they cleaned up the glass, and Jake covered the window as best he could for the night. "There, that should be safe enough, being on the second floor. I'll have it replaced tomorrow." He smiled at Julianne to assure her it would be all right. He went outside and checked the perimeter and the street out front. Satisfied no one was there, he set the alarm and went upstairs.

Julianne was already in her nightclothes. "I'm so tired. Do you mind if I sleep with you again tonight? I'm still a little shaken."

"I wouldn't have it any other way." Jake turned the lights out, and they headed for his bedroom. Julianne crawled under the sheet and into the comfort of Jake's bed, while he went to the bathroom for his shower. "I won't be long," he said. By the time he came out, Julianne was sound asleep. Jake smiled and climbed into bed beside her. Sleep didn't come easy for him. His head was going in circles trying to think of what to do about Jordan, not to mention the room was still all lit up by the police lights outside. The police were still scouring the bushes where the shooter had been hiding.

As they were having their coffee the next morning, Julianne asked Jake, "Wouldn't what happened last night add some credence to the tape you took to the police?"

"Maybe it would, I'll go today and talk to the Captain again.

She shrugged her shoulders and placed a call to Jordan explaining what had happened last night and that she wouldn't be coming back until they caught the person responsible. She was carefully choosing her words so as not to appear to be pointing a finger at him, just yet. She and Jake had decided to play dumb to knowing Jordan was responsible by making him think they thought the gunman was after Jake because of his business.

"Julianne, that's terrible, and I am so sorry," Jordan said, all the while trying to keep his anger under control. He would deal with Blake immediately. "But I'm afraid I don't see the connection between what happened and your coming to work. You would be perfectly safe while here. We have impeccable security on the premises."

"I understand that, Jordan, but I feel it's best if I just keep a low profile for awhile. It will be safer that way. I promise I will let you know if there are any changes. I hope when this is resolved we can pick up where we left off."

"Of course we can. I hope the person who did this is captured very soon. In the meantime, you stay alert and safe, and hopefully we will see you soon." Jordan replied.

"Thank you for your concern, Jordan. I'll check in with you in a few days." Julianne said good-bye.

A Stranger in the Will

"I have the feeling his hired gun went out of bounds here. Did you hear the tension in his voice? He was trying very hard to tamp down his anger over something," Jake stated.

"Well, I'll give it a week or so and see how it goes. If nothing happens maybe I'll go back and see if my presence ramps things up again."

"Oh, that makes a lot of sense. Are you saying if they don't kill you within this next week you'll go fuel the fire some more?" Jake was madder than hell that she even said that.

Julianne walked over to look out what little glass was left in the living room window. "I can't stay hidden for the rest of my life, Jake. Something has to force Jordan to make his move so we can get this over with."

THIRTY-FOUR

Jordan hung up with Julianne and immediately dialed Blake.

He was so mad he could barely push the numbers on the phone, his hands were shaking with anger.

Blake noticed it was Jordan on caller ID. She was expecting him to call, so she braced herself. "Hello, Jordan."

"Blake, didn't you understand the sequence you were suppose to stick to? What the hell were you doing? I specifically told you Ivan first, did I not? Do you not understand English? I am so angry right now I can't even think. You be in my office Thursday morning, first thing." Jordan slammed the phone down.

Blake knew he would be mad, but he was way beyond mad. Not much scared her, but the tone of Jordan's voice was a little unsettling. Just as she was wondering if she should ditch this job, her off the charts computer beeped to alert her that Ivan had surfaced. It was Tuesday, so she had one day to get this done.

The sooner she got started the better her chances of having good news for Jordan on Thursday.

Ivan had opened a new bank account at a Huntington Beach bank. *Well, well*, she thought. *Thank you Ivan! I do believe your stupidity just saved my ass with Jordan.* She sat and began to explore her computer to see if she could find Ivan.

A Stranger in the Will

She found the address of the Huntington Beach bank where he had opened his account.
Hmm, she thought, *maybe I'll just take a little ride around the area to see if I spot him.*

Very excited, she grabbed her bag and her keys and headed for the door. She drove to Huntington Beach, found the bank, and went inside in hopes he would be there, but no such luck.

Being lunchtime, she decided to walk across the street and have a bite to eat before anymore searching. She got her lunch and sat on the deck. It was a beautiful day to people watch and enjoy the ocean. She took a bite of her fries and almost choked as she spotted a man walking a dog on the beach. The man looked an awful lot like Ivan from a distance. Grabbing her drink and burger, she ran down the stairs onto the beach to follow him. She caught up with him and started to pass. She stopped to speak to Ivan about how cute the dog was, asking if she could pet him. "What's his name?"

"Sure, you can pet him, he loves attention. His name is Oscar. Fitting for southern California, don't you think?" Ivan smiled at her.

"That's very cute," she said. "How long have you had him?"

"Just got him yesterday. You never know when you need one for protection these days."

"How true that is," Blake said as she smiled. "I'm checking out the area myself. I'm thinking of moving here. Do you mind if I walk with you and pick your brain about the place for a few minutes?"

"Not at all, but I just moved here myself about two weeks ago. I don't know how much help I'll be."

"Well, at least two weeks worth," she laughed. Ivan smiled as they started to walk. Blake asked questions she thought someone thinking of moving here would ask. Ivan could answer some and not others. "Do you know of any decent apartments for rent around here?"

"The place I moved into is very nice. It's clean, quiet, and seems pretty safe."

"Maybe I should take a look at them. That's a start, anyway."

"I'm just about ready to head home. If you're ready, you can follow me, or I can give you the address to check it out later."

"I can go now, if that's no trouble for you. My car is parked right down the street from Huntington Bank."

"That's great, and if you need a bank, that's a great one." Ivan said. Blake just smiled as they headed for their cars. Blake pointed to her car, and Ivan told her his was just a couple of cars up. "You follow me, and I'll watch in the rearview so I don't lose you." Blake thanked him as she got in her car, all the time thinking this was way too easy.

Ivan walked back and tapped on her window. "What's your name?" He asked as she rolled down the window. "Mine is Ivan."

Blake extended her hand. "It's nice to meet you Ivan. My name is Blake." She saw no reason to give him a fake name, he wouldn't be around much longer to tell anybody.

Tonight, this contract would be finished.

THIRTY-FIVE

Blake followed Ivan into the parking lot of the apartment complex, all the while checking for security cameras or any other security they might use. Ivan motioned for her to pull in next to his car, that being his second allotted spot. As they entered his first floor apartment, she noticed it was bright and cheery. Ivan took her on a tour of the two bedroom, two bath unit. He explained they did have one bedroom apartments also. Blake was trying to act extremely interested. "I can take you down and introduce you to the office staff, and you can fill out the application, if you want."

"Oh, I'm not sure I'm ready for that yet. I have more research to do before I decide this is the place for me. But thank you for all your help today. I really appreciate it. You have helped me a lot."

"You're welcome," Ivan said as he walked her to the door. "Do you know how to get back to the highway from here?"

"I think so," she said, as she headed back to her own car with her mind racing over the excitement of completing this part of the job. *Jordan will be much happier when I see him Thursday, for tonight I will take care of his first priority.*

She arrived home with plenty of time left to plan her attack and carry it out. All of the things needed were gathered in a duffel bag in the closet. she dragged it out and removed her black outfit, vest, and ski mask. She opened a hidden compartment in the back of the closet and dug out her hand gun and ammo. Laying it all out on the table, she decided to take a shower and nap and leave around one o'clock in the morning.

It was 1:39 a.m. when Blake pulled into Ivan's parking lot, scoping the area for residents that might be outside or have lights on in their units, signaling they were up. Everything was quiet, as it should be for that hour of the morning. Heading out to the back of Ivan's unit, she made last minute checks of her equipment. *Okay, here we go.*

First thing out was her tranquilizer gun as she jimmied open the slider. The dog was growling, but not barking, so she hit him with a dart. Down Oscar went on the dining room floor, sleeping like a baby. She slid the door open enough to squeeze through. While there earlier, she had taken notice there were no alarms around the doors or windows. She was confident that was not a problem. She had no idea Ivan had installed a laser beam that triggered a quiet alarm in his room.

She went down the short hallway to his bedroom door. Turning the knob as quietly as she could, she opened the door and came face to face with his extended arm and a gun. Shock came over her for a split second, and she started backing up with her gun pointing at Ivan.

"Stay calm, buddy, just money I'm after. No need to go overboard here." Ivan recognized the voice.

"Blake, what are you doing?"

"Blake who?" She said as she tried to change her voice in panic.

Damn, she thought, *I should have used a fake name after all.*

"What'd you do with the dog?"

"Just tranq'd him, he'll be fine in awhile."

"I don't keep money in the house, so I'm afraid you picked on the wrong place, lady. Take the mask off."

"Not a chance." Blake fired her gun, grazing his arm. He fell back just enough to afford her the time she needed to get out. She got to her car and was gone before he recovered and ran after her.

A Stranger in the Will

THIRTY-SIX

"Hey buddy, any chance you can come over for a little powwow and update?" Jake asked when Nick answered his phone. Nick told him he wouldn't be able to come until the end of his shift. He told Jake he had gone back to work a couple of days ago. Julianne suggested they do this over dinner, and Nick was all for that. He didn't know about the shooting yet, so he was in for a surprise. As Jake hung up, his phone rang again.

"Jake, this is Ivan Slater. Jordan sent someone after me. I'm sure of it."

"Where are you?" Jake asked.

"In my apartment in Huntington Beach. She broke into my apartment early this morning."

"Ivan, what the hell are you doing in Huntington Beach? You're supposed to be far away from here."

"I'll explain when I see you, but I need to come over now. I haven't even called the police yet."

"Don't call the police, get your ass over here, I'm sure you remember the way." Jake said sarcastically. As Jake put the phone down, he explained to Julianne what Ivan had said.
"Julianne, he said it was a girl. Remember I said the footprints looked like a girls."

"Jake, this is getting out of hand. Jordan won't stop until he gets both of us. Ivan isn't safe living here, didn't he understand that? He must have known his life wouldn't be worth anything after I surfaced and Jordan realized he'd been had."

"I don't have any idea what Ivan's doing. He had to know this would happen. The stupid...Jake didn't finish. I'd better go down and tell Donna he's coming so she doesn't panic when he walks in."

"That would be a good idea," Julianne said.

Jake went downstairs as Julianne started dinner, setting a place for Ivan too.

"Donna, why don't you pack up and go home early. I'll cover until five o'clock. Ivan is coming over, he didn't leave town, and I don't want you here when he comes in."

"If that's the case, you can't get me out of here fast enough." She grabbed her purse and hustled out the door.

Nick showed up first. He had wanted to see Donna to make sure she was okay. Jake explained that he let her go home early, that Ivan was on his way over, and what Ivan had said. He also brought him up to date on the shooting the night before.

Ivan rang the bell, and Nick pushed Jake aside saying, "Allow me." He opened the door, and Ivan didn't stand a chance. Nick decked Ivan with a hard right to the jaw. "That's for Donna and what you tried to do to me and my friends. This discussion tonight could not go on without a down payment toward settling the score between us. Why are you still around here, anyway? You have a death wish?"

A Stranger in the Will

Jake let out a little snicker over what Nick did.

The three men then headed upstairs. Julianne had set out beers for them before dinner, for the men needed them to calm down. They all took a seat in the living room, while Ivan began to tell them what happened earlier this morning. When he finished, Jake told him how lucky he was that he put that laser tripwire in. "We told you what would happen if you didn't get far away from here. Why didn't you leave?"

"I did, but as I was trying to find someplace to go, I realized I didn't want to leave L.A.. I've been here all my life. I figured if I went to Huntington Beach, I would never run into anyone in Jordan's circles." He told Jake about Blake approaching him at the beach during the day, how it all went down, and that he thought that was who broke into his apartment. "I recognized her voice, and then she hurriedly tried to change it."

"It probably was, and there's a good possibility she was hired by Jordan." Jake went on to tell Ivan what happened yesterday with the shooting and how he found small footprints, more than likely female. "Ivan, you can't stay around here.

Jordan will keep at it until he succeeds. He is very angry that you betrayed him. You have to leave until he is locked up. You call me now and then, and I'll let you know if it's safe to come back."

"Do you think Blake will try again, knowing I have an alarm system?"

"No, Ivan, she probably wouldn't go back to your apartment. She'll just pick you off in a crowd next time," Nick said, as he shook his head in disbelief.

"How am I supposed to close out my bank account and get my things to my car without getting shot?"

"I'll come over when you're ready and stand guard, but you have to have all your stuff ready to go as soon as the bank opens in the morning. Call when you're ready. After we load your car, we'll go to the bank in my car, then back here to pick up yours. I'll follow you out to the edge of town to make sure you're not being followed, and you'll be on your way from there alone. Don't be an idiot, get as far away as you can this time."

"Okay, and thank you, Jake. I'm sorry I got involved in this to begin with. After all I tried to do to you guys, I can't believe you're helping me. I promise I'll keep in touch so you know how to get me when Jordan goes to trial. I'll come back to testify."

"Nick and I will follow you home right after dinner. Once you're in you stay in for the night." When dinner was done Jake asked Julianne if she was ready. He wasn't leaving her home alone.

Once Ivan was safely inside his apartment, they went back home. Nick told Jake to call if he needed him and left.

THIRTY-SEVEN

Julianne had slept in her own room all night. She knew it was time to stop relying on Jake so much and to get back to taking care of herself. However, she had to admit she missed the warmth and security of having him next to her.

The next morning, Jake stood in the kitchen doorway, staring at Julianne as she made coffee, disappointed as well that she had not been with him last night. "Good morning," he said.

A bit startled, she turned toward him and smiled. "Good morning! How long have you been standing there?"

"Just a minute. I was enjoying the view." He put his arms around her and whispered that he missed her last night. She pulled back so she could look into his eyes and acknowledged the same. "Good, let's not do that again." The twinkle in her eyes told him she agreed.

Donna knocked on the apartment door, ready for her morning coffee with them. "How'd it go last night with Ivan?" she asked, as she took her cup to the table. Jake proceeded to fill her in on what happened to Ivan and the plan for getting him out of town today.

"The further the better, as far as I'm concerned," she stated.

"Donna, Ivan asked me to give this to you this morning. I have no idea what it is, so if you would like me to open it, I will." Jake handed Donna an envelope. Her hand was shaking as she reached for it. She removed the short note enclosed with a check folded inside. She gasped at the amount of the check. She couldn't read the note, so she handed it back to Jake with the check. Jake and Julianne were also taken back by the amount. Jake started to read the letter aloud:

Donna,
I know this check will never erase the horror you must have felt that night. I know saying I'm sorry would never be enough, but, Donna, I am so very sorry. Meeting all of you has changed me. I am ashamed of what I tried to do. If it's any consolation, my life has changed for the better because of all of you. I will never do such a thing to anyone again. Please accept my apology and this check. I hope it will help to make life a little better for you."

Ivan

Jake folded the letter and handed it back to Donna as he said, "well I'll be damned. Who would have ever thought?" I think you should take some more time off so you and Brad can take a nice vacation with part of that $20,000.00. You've certainly earned it."

A Stranger in the Will

Donna was holding the envelope, still dumbstruck. "Why don't you go back home and catch Brad before he leaves? He certainly doesn't need to hang around the corner today waiting for a job truck to come along." Donna stood and hugged Jake and Julianne. She ran for the door, her heart was aching to get home and tell her husband.

She turned back to Jake, "This is real, isn't it?"
"I'd bet it is," Jake responded. As Donna closed the apartment door, Julianne started to laugh when she heard Donna bounding down the stairs.
The phone rang, breaking their concentration on Donna. "Jake Matthews," he answered.
"Jake, it's Ivan. I'm all packed and ready to load the car. Since I backed up right to my door last night, I think I'm okay to go between the door and the trunk. I looked out the front window and didn't see anything suspicious."
"Ivan, you just wait. There are too many trees across the street. We'll be there shortly, and stay away from the window." Ivan agreed to wait, though he didn't feel it necessary."

Ivan waved to Julianne as they pulled into the parking space next to his car. Julianne waved back, all the while thinking Ivan still didn't get it, he was standing in an open window.

Jake exited his car under the cover of Ivan's. He told Julianne to wait until he checked out the area. When all was clear, Julianne went into Ivan's apartment. Jake stayed outside, constantly sweeping the area, while the other two loaded Ivan's car. When they finished, the three of them left in Jake's car to take care of the banking. Ivan cleared out his account of the $90,000 left out of

the $100,000.00 he had gotten from Julianne and Jordan combined.

Ivan gave Jake $20,000. "Give this to Donna, and tear up the check. I didn't leave anything in the account to cover it." Jake agreed to do that as he called Donna to tell her not to cash the check, since he had the cash for it.

Ivan got out of the car with his keys in hand. He put the key into his lock as Jake heard the bullet leave what he could only assume was Blake's rifle barrel. He watched Ivan fall as he yelled to Julianne to get down in the front seat. Jake ran full throttle in a zigzag pattern to the tree line. Gun drawn, he searched, but Blake was gone. He hurried back to Ivan. He kneeled down to find where the bullet entered. Ivan was breathing hard and knew he wouldn't make it. "Jake, take the rest of the money and do something good with it for me. Get it before it becomes evidence."

"Okay, buddy, I will."

Julianne was now kneeling next to Jake and holding Ivan's hand.

"I'm so sor..." his voice trailed off, as he gasped one last time, and it was over. Jake called the police, but before they arrived he needed to get the money out of Ivan's pocket.

All reports and statements taken left out the trip to the bank. Ivan was taken away, and Jake assured the police he would take care of the burial and any other expenses.

Jake then called Donna and told her what happened to Ivan and that they were on their way home, in case she wanted to meet them now to make the swap. Both cars pulled into Jake's driveway at the same time.

Donna gave Jake the check and watched as he tore it up and handed her the cash. "After what Ivan did to me, I can't say I feel bad that he's dead, but I am grateful for this," she said as she waved the money in front of her.

"That's perfectly understandable to feel that way, but I do believe he was sincere when he apologized."

"I do, too." Julianne said.

"Oh, I do also, but I can't forgive him. My nightmares won't let me."

Brad took his wife's hand to comfort her as they started back to their car. Julianne stopped her as she passed by, hugging Donna and telling her how sorry she was that her being there caused her such pain. Donna rubbed Julianne's arm and smiled as she and Brad got into their car.

THIRTY-EIGHT

Blake arrived at Simms Trading first thing the next morning as Jordan had ordered. She was escorted to his office immediately.

"Good morning, Jordan," she said in her usual sassy tone. "Did you see the news last night?"

"I did, and I want to hear all the details. But, before we begin, I have something to say."

Blake noticed the anger in Jordan's eyes. At that point she knew her accomplishment last night was not getting her out of trouble for going off on her own.

"Don't you ever go against my wishes again, Blake. I spent a lot of time putting a plan in place, and I can't afford to have you or anyone else screwing it up. There are plenty of people out there who do what you do, and I won't hesitate to make the change. I left no room for error. You got that?"

"I got it." Blake felt her own anger building at being scolded like a child. She hadn't liked Jordan the first time they met, but, for the money, she thought she could handle him.

"Now, tell me what happened last night."

Blake proceeded to tell Jordan how she originally found Ivan by going to Long Beach and spotting and following him on the beach. She then explained how they started talking about living in the area and so he took her to his apartment complex to show her what she could get for her

A Stranger in the Will

money. "Then, I went back that night and broke into his apartment. The only problem was he had jerry rigged a tripwire across the slider into his dining room. The alarm was set to quietly go off in his bedroom, and he met me with a revolver when I opened his door. I shot him and grazed his arm, and he fell back long enough to allow me to get away. The next day I went back and spent the day in the trees across from his apartment. Low and behold, Julianne drove in with her P.I. in tow. He stayed outside sweeping the area looking for me, he even passed under the tree I had climbed. Julianne helped Ivan pack up his car, and then they all left in the P.I.'s car. I waited until they pulled in again about an hour later. When Ivan stepped out, I picked him off, real clean. The P.I. yelled for Julianne to get down in the car as he started running to the trees, zigzagging to make it harder to shoot him. When he didn't find me he ran back to where Ivan was lying. The lady was already on her knees holding his hand, and she started talking to him. I climbed down from the tree and left before the police got there. That's it."

"Excellent," Jordan said. "Now, keep in mind what I hired you to do to Ivan because he crossed me. No more making your own decisions because you think you have a better idea."

"I won't, and I'm sorry for doing that." So what's the plan now? I go after the girl and the P.I.?"

"The P.I.'s name is Jake Matthews, and no, I told you I would take care of Julianne myself. You can take care of Jake anytime.

Here is the next installment." Jordan slid an envelope across his desk. "Let me know when it's done, and stick to the game plan this time."

Blake reached across and collected her envelope. She stood, thanked Jordan, and turned to leave.

"Keep it clean and untraceable," Jordan reminded her. "If you get caught, you're on your own." Blake just nodded as she closed his door.

What an ass! Maybe when I'm done, I'll waste him. She laughed to herself, *thinking that after she was paid in full, she'd take care of Jordan just for the satisfaction. This one would be on the house. The expression on his face would be payment enough.*

On the way home Blake picked up a pizza and beer. It was time to put together her plans for Jake.

Meanwhile, Jake had the feeling that Jordan was stepping up the game to a dangerous level for Julianne. Blake could be showing up here again at any time. He decided it would be best to get a temp in and get Julianne out of the front office while Donna was gone. Now all he had to do was present the idea to Julianne knowing it would not be well received.

A Stranger in the Will

THIRTY-NINE

Kylie knocked on Jordan's door, stepped inside, and sat in a chair facing him. "Jordan, what's the latest on Julianne? Is she coming back?" Kylie asked how far Blake had been ordered to go and what her brother was up to. She had no idea things had already gone so far. She noticed the strange look on his face and, she knew that smirky look wasn't funny. "Oh Jordan, what have you done to her?"

"Nothing yet, my dear sister. Blake has taken care of Ivan for betraying us, but I told her Julianne was mine. However, she could have the P.I."

"Excuse me, but there is no us. You have sole credit for this little scheme of yours. I did not agree to any of it, and I'm not taking the fall with you."

"Oh, but you would, Kylie. You may not have planned any of it, but you were and are very much aware of the ultimate outcome I'm after."

"Jordan, all I was aware of is that you were trying to scare Julianne off and away from Simms Trading. I knew nothing about murdering anybody, and I want no part in anybody getting killed. I thought you were just going to scare Ivan into returning money you lent him."

"Kylie, he took $50,000 from me for a job he didn't do. I wasn't going to allow him to just walk away."

"Oh man, Jordan, you're out of control. This is insane." Kylie got up and headed for the door. "You have to stop this now, Jordan, it's going to backfire in your face."

Jordan yelled for her to come back as she shut the door. Kylie was shaking all the way back to her office. She shut her door, sat down behind her desk, and dropped her face in her hands as she tried to deal with what she had just learned.

A Stranger in the Will

FORTY

Jake called Julianne into his office to tell her he was going to hire a temp. She didn't disappoint him with her reaction, but he noticed she seemed to be lacking the conviction in her tone this time.

"Julianne," he said, "I expected an all out battle. What's wrong?"

Just then they heard the office door open. Julianne went to see who came in.

"Kylie!" she said with surprise. The hair on the back of Jake's neck went up at the mention of her name. He stepped into the doorway of his office, ready for anything.

"Julianne, we need to talk. Jordan is out of his mind, and I'm afraid of what he might do to keep you out of the company."

Jake motioned for both women to come into his office and sit at the small conference table. Julianne shrugged her shoulders inquisitively toward Jake as she passed in front of him.

"I don't know where to begin," Kylie said as she pulled out her chair. "I knew Jordan was very angry at the reading of our father's will, but I never thought he would be considering murder. He had a woman named Blake kill Ivan Slater. She's going to come after you, Jake. Julianne I'm afraid for you. He's instructed Blake to leave you alone, he's saving *you* for himself." Julianne looked at Jake, wondering if he was thinking this is what they needed to take to the police. Her question was answered when he spoke.

"Kylie, are you willing to tell the police what you just told us? This is the information we need to convince them that your brother is a dangerous man."

"You're kidding me, right? I only came here to warn you. He's my brother. I don't want him arrested. You've got to talk to him and stop him before he gets in any deeper."

"Which one of us do you suppose he would listen to, Kylie?" Jake said with a note of sarcasm. "If he's gone far enough to come after us in Tahoe and now has had Ivan killed, I think it's already a little late for a chat."

"What are you talking about? When did he come after you in Tahoe?"

"Kylie, didn't you know what he paid Ivan the money for? It wasn't because they were best buddies. He sent Ivan to kill us while we were staying at the lake house your father left Julianne."

Kylie gasped. "That's what Jordan meant when he said Ivan took money from him for a job he didn't do. No, I didn't know anything about that. I thought he gave Ivan a loan to get out of some financial trouble. Oh my God, he's already gone over the edge. What can we do now?"

"If you can't bring yourself to go to the police, will you at least help us to get him before he kills anyone else?"

"Listen, I have to go. If he finds out I was here, who knows what he'd do to me. I'm his sister, but even I won't be safe anywhere if he thinks I betrayed him." Kylie pushed back her chair and stood staring at Julianne. "I'm sorry, but maybe it would be best for your safety if you didn't come back. Maybe then he won't feel it necessary to continue this behavior." Kylie hurried out of Jake's office before she could change her mind.

"What's our next move Jake? We really could have used her help."

"I'm not sure, maybe I'll take another shot at her and try to convince her how much of a danger Jordan is to anyone who crosses him, including her."

"She seems to already suspect that. Maybe I should go back to work with her. We'd be spending a lot of time behind closed doors in her office. That might be the only opportunity to talk privately with her. I know it's a risk, Jake, but someone has to shake things up, or this could go on forever. This is the perfect chance for me to have a purpose in my life. Being part owner of a company like Simms Trading would set me up for life and help me know what kind of a man my father was. I'm not ready to give that up."

"What do you think about you and me seeing if we can arrange a little chat with Madeline to see where she stands in all this? We could arrange that through Christopher Romano." Jake said as he raised an eyebrow to Julianne.

"Interesting thought, but do you really think she'd be willing to talk to us? Jordan is her son, after all. I love the idea if she'd do it, but we'd have to be prepared for it to backfire, too."

"That's very true," Jake answered, " but do you think it's worth a shot?"

"I honestly don't think we'll get very far, but I suppose it's worth a try. I'll lock up and get ready for dinner while you call Christopher."

As Julianne was heading for the front office, Jake pulled her to him, holding her tight as he tried to reassure her without making promises he wasn't sure he could keep.

A Stranger in the Will

FORTY-ONE

Jake placed the call to Christopher Romano's office and was taken by surprise when the attorney himself answered.

"Mr. Romano," Jake said, "this is Jake Matthews. Julianne and I would like to talk to you about concerns we have about Jordan. Is there a time you can clear your schedule rather quickly? It's important."

Romano cleared his throat, trying to hide his uneasiness about what they had to say. "Hold on Jake, let me check my schedule."

He pushed the hold button, sat back in his chair, and ran his hands through his hair in frustration. Somehow he always felt this time would come. Jordan Simms was a real problem. He was sure Conrad's apprehension about his children was well founded. Christopher got back on the phone and apologized for the wait.

"Jake, I can see you and Ms. Sullivan tomorrow at four o'clock if this won't take longer than an hour. I have a previous engagement at five thirty."

"That's great, we'll be there and thank you very much. You have a good night," Jake said as he hung up. He headed upstairs, after checking the alarm, to inform Julianne.

Jake opened the door to his apartment and the smell of what Julianne was fixing for dinner filled the air. He wasn't sure what it was, but then he didn't care, he just wanted to dig in.

"That smells wonderful," he told her as he wrapped his arms around her waist.

He stabbed a fork into the pan, catching a chunk of tender, flaky fish. He went for seconds and quickly got his hand slapped.

"Sit," Julianne scolded as she began to dish up his plate.

Jake laughed as he gave her a peck on her cheek. Lately, he was finding himself amazed at the little things he didn't know he was missing by not having a woman in his life. Jake waited for Julianne to sit before he started telling her about his call to the attorney.

"We have an appointment tomorrow at four o'clock. We have to be prepared and remember everything we need to discuss because, he only has an hour."

"I guess after dinner we need to sit down and make a list then. You know as well as I do that once we get started discussing things, we'll forget something," Julianne replied.

"Good idea."

They ate pretty much in silence, both their minds working overtime. Julianne wondered what good would come from this meeting with Romano, while Jake wondered about mentioning his suspicions of a possible leak in the attorney's office.

As Julianne cleaned the table, Jake went to his office to retrieve paper and pencils. Each sitting at opposite ends of the sofa, with pencils in hand, they began to write. By the time they were done,

A Stranger in the Will

each list was equally about as long. They compared and, to neither one's surprise, the lists were almost identical. They made a few adjustments and came up with one good list.

Julianne stood and stretched. "I think I'll head off to bed. I don't know why I'm so tired tonight." She said goodnight and told Jake she would see him in the morning,

"Goodnight, Julianne," Jake replied with disappointment on his face. He wondered what was up with her tonight. She seemed distant, and he was very concerned, hoping all of this wasn't causing her to reconsider going back to Singapore. He made a mental note to talk to her about it in the morning. Jake shut the lights off and went to his room, already feeling a bit rejected and afraid of losing her.

FORTY-TWO

Jake woke the next morning to noises he was not used to hearing. Retrieving his gun from the nightstand, he quietly opened his bedroom door. The memories of the Lake Tahoe incident came rushing in. Once again he peeked out his door and saw a small light in the kitchen. In a moment of déjà vu, he plastered himself to the hallway wall as he headed toward the small light in his otherwise dark apartment.

"Julianne!" he gasped, as he lowered his gun. "What are you doing?"

"Jake! Oh my God, you scared me. Why do you have your gun?"

"I heard noises out here. I'm sorry I startled you. What are doing up at four o'clock?"

"I couldn't sleep. Jake, this is all so crazy. I was going to tell you that I was packing to go back to Singapore. I should never have broken my promise to my mother. She obviously knew something she was afraid to tell me."

Jake set his gun on the table and took Julianne into his arms. He started to whisper to her that this is what he feared was happening. He told her how he wondered last night, as she headed for her bedroom, if all of this was getting to be too much and how, he planned on trying to talk about it this morning.

"Jake, you have done so much for me. You did what I hired you to do, but I should have left it at that. What happened to Donna and Ivan, and then us almost getting shot...I don't think I can do this anymore. I have the house and the money. I can live off that and probably get my job back in Singapore. Or maybe even go to settle with my relatives in Denver."

Jake let his arms slip from around her as he stared into her eyes in total disbelief. "Julianne? Doesn't what we started here between us mean anything? I thought you knew how I felt about you and, honestly, I thought you had feelings for me, too. I think it's a little early to call it love, but hell, I'm falling in love with you."

"Jake, you have to understand, it's because of my feelings for you that I have to get as far away from here as I can. I would never forgive myself if anything happened to you at all, let alone because of me."

"Listen to me, we went through this when Donna was hurt. I told you then that it wouldn't make any difference. I am going to settle the score with Jordan even if you leave. Because of Donna, he made it personal. I will still get him for that, and more so if he causes me to lose you."

"Jake, I'm so scared. I don't know what to do anymore."

Jake took Julianne's hand, guiding her into the living room to sit down and talk. That's when he spotted her suitcases. He whirled around with fury in his eyes. "You were going to leave without telling me! Did you plan on leaving me a note, or just walking out the door?"

"I wasn't leaving until you got up, then I would explain. I'm not totally heartless! I owe you a lot, Jake. No one knows that more than I do."

She grabbed a napkin from the table to wipe her eyes, the tears now running uncontrollably down her cheeks.

Jake held her hand as he walked her to the sofa, where they sat embracing each other without speaking and, finally fell asleep.

Jake opened his eyes at six o'clock, but Julianne was gone. He looked over to where her suitcases had almost tripped him, and they were also gone. His heart was in his throat until he heard the shower running.

A Stranger in the Will

FORTY-THREE

Christopher Romano stood as Jake escorted Julianne into his office. They all shook hands, while Jake thanked the attorney for seeing them on short notice.

"Jake and Julianne, please allow me to start by telling you how sorry I am that Jordan is not doing as his father had hoped."

He looked at Julianne. "Your father was a kind man, and he knew there would be problems with Jordan more so than Kylie. However, she can be manipulated, hence, the reason for the stipulations in the will that they don't cause any problems. They could lose everything.

"Making Jordan even a bigger threat to her," Jake inserted.

"I would think so. Now we have to decide what to do, so why don't you two start from the beginning."

Julianne took out the list they had made up last night and handed the attorney a copy so he could follow along.

"Wow," Romano said as he quickly skimmed down the list. "These are some pretty heavy accusations. Any proof?"

"The only one we can prove is the contract put out on Julianne. We caught Ivan, the man Jordan hired for the hit, red-handed at the Tahoe house."

Jake proceeded to tell Romano the details of the deal they made with Ivan to get the tape.

"We have the tape. The other details are ones we simply know. However, Kylie also knows, to a certain extent. Whether she'll talk is another story.

"I took the tape and our story to the police. Do you have any idea how connected Jordan Simms is? They accused me of fabricating it."

"Wait," the attorney said. "I have a question before we go any further. I want to know how Jordan knew you would be at the Tahoe house."

Jake looked at Julianne. "Now's a good a time as any to approach something else I wanted to talk to you about," Jake said.

"I think we have to discuss the possibility of a leak in your office, Mr. Romano. Before you say anything, please hear me out. I found that Jordan had gone for an overnight trip to Singapore while Julianne's mother was dying. We think he went to see her and to warn Julianne to stay away from her father or his family. How else would he have known about Julianne and her mother? He may even be aware we are here now."

"Are you sure, Jake? I shudder to think anyone would betray me like that. However, I will start an investigation first thing in the morning. Now, back to these other allegations."

"Okay," Jake said, "we know that Jordan hired another hitter. This one is a woman, and she's taking Ivan's place after he found out Ivan betrayed him by not killing Julianne in Tahoe. That woman killed Ivan. We also believe she is responsible for firing a shot into my living room.

A Stranger in the Will

Here's a copy of the police report." Jake reached across the desk and handed it to Romano.

"Ivan had told us of a lady named Blake catching him on the beach. Pretending she was moving to Huntington Beach, she engaged him in conversation. She followed him back to his apartment again, pretending to be interested in them for herself. According to Ivan she came back that night and tried to shoot him. She did get off a shot that grazed his shoulder, but she didn't succeed in killing him until the next morning. Julianne and I were there when he was shot.

"I can't believe Jordan has gone this far. I will bring Madeline, Jordan, and Kylie in here to discuss this with them. I will call Mrs. Simms first thing in the morning. I'm sorry, I have to cut this short, unfortunately I can't cancel my 5:30 appointment tonight."

"Before you call them all in here, we had given some thought," Jake motioned between himself and Julianne, "to maybe talking to Madeline alone. She might have some ideas regarding how to go about this. If you think there's any chance she'd cooperate, that is"

"I don't know Mrs. Simms as well as I did your father," the attorney said as he looked at Julianne, "but I certainly think it's worth a try. I'll call her to set up an appointment and let you know, Julianne. If Jordan is waiting for you to come back to work, Julianne, I doubt he will try anything else before then. Nonetheless, please be careful and stay alert. I will also notify you if or when I find someone on my staff who has betrayed our confidences. Thank you for bringing that to my attention."

Julianne stood to shake hands, as did Jake. "Thank you. We hope you get somewhere with this, but I have my doubts," Jake said.

A Stranger in the Will

FORTY-FOUR

The following morning Christopher Romano decided his first priority was to find the person responsible for the obvious leaks coming out of his office. The way to go about that would be a difficult process. He knew he couldn't directly accuse any particular person. However, he knew that bringing them in one by one to question them would look like he was doing just that. Unfortunately, the urgency of the matter left no time to proceed any other way.

He also knew he had to place that call to Madeline Simms.

He started to reminisce about many years ago when Conrad Simms came to him. Conrad wanted a lawyer who could be there to help and guide him as he began to build Simms Trading. It wasn't something he had wanted to venture into, Romano remembered.

I should have listened to my instincts back then, he thought. *This is turning into a nightmare.*

Christopher placed the call to Madeline, explaining as little as possible as to why he wanted to see her, he said just enough to get her to come in.
The appointment was set for three o'clock that afternoon.

Romano, having an idea who the leak could be, decided to start with his receptionist, Erin. For some time he had noticed her attire and jewelry were a bit beyond her means. Chances were, he was about to confirm what he now felt sure of.

Erin was at her desk, very busy filing her nails. Startled, she jumped as she heard her boss call he name over the intercom.

"Erin, can I see you in my office, please?"

"Sure, Mr. Romano, give me a minute?"

"Now, Erin!" Her boss commanded.

Erin spoke back to the intercom. "Yes, sir, she replied as she grabbed her purse from the drawer and a few miscellaneous things off her desk. Briskly, she walked out the door toward the elevator. With a knot in her stomach, she knew he had somehow found out about her arrangement with Jordan Simms. But how? She questioned as she hurriedly exited the elevator on the first floor and ran out of the building to the street.

Romano stepped out from behind his desk and was buttoning his suit jacket as he walked toward his office door and out to reception.

Erin was not there. Opening the office door, he searched the hall and looked toward the elevators. He went back to his office and dialed security at the front entrance.

"This is Attorney Romano on four. Can you tell me if a young lady with long blonde hair, wearing a yellow and black dress, just left the building?"

"Do you mean Erin?" the guard asked.

"Yes," Romano answered.

A Stranger in the Will

"Yeah," the guard said. "In quite a hurry, she didn't even scan her badge out."

"Thank you," Romano said as he hung up.

He then placed a call to the police. He explained what just happened, telling them he suspected she violated his attorney/client privilege and the confidentiality agreement she signed upon her hire. He wanted her picked up for questioning and, should she be found to be guilty of these accusations, he would be pressing charges.

He felt, at this point, he could move on to something else. There was no need to continue his search, he was confident he had found the breach.

FORTY-FIVE

At three o'clock sharp, Madeline Simms entered Christopher Romano's reception area with her usual uppity stride. Romano's secretary, Sarah, who was filling in until they replaced Erin, saw Madeline walk right past her, heading to Romano's office.

"Excuse me, Mrs. Simms, you'll have to wait a moment. Mr. Romano is on a call right now. He should be finished very soon."

Madeline strolled over to the seating area and sat down with a huff.

It took only a couple of minutes before Romano came to reception and greeted Madeline. He acknowledged he was ready for her by raising his hand to indicate she could proceed down the hall.

"Christopher, what's this about? You were very vague on the telephone this morning."

"Madeline, thank you for coming so soon. This is a matter of some urgency, but I didn't want to alarm you prematurely. Some rather disturbing issues have been brought to my attention regarding Jordan's behavior toward Julianne."

"Such as?" she inquired, with a bit of sarcasm.

"Please have a seat." He motioned to the chair facing his desk.

"Madeline, some very disturbing accusations were brought to my attention yesterday. We need to discuss them and a possible course of action, if

A Stranger in the Will

they are true, to stop Jordan, before he ends up in prison, or worse."

"Christopher, what on earth are you talking about?" Madeline's expression suggested, he tread lightly.

"Madeline, I don't know how to begin without upsetting you, so I'm just going to have to lay it out. Julianne and Jake Matthews, Jake is the private investigator Julianne hired to find Conrad, if you recall, came to see me yesterday. Jordan apparently had hired a 'hit man', if you will, to kill Julianne." Romano waited for her to comprehend what he had told her. He then handed her a copy of the list Julianne and Jake had given him. He could see the devastation on her face as she read down the list, holding her hand over her heart.

"Oh my Lord, Christopher. I know Jordan can be a bit combative, but this is not possible. I can't believe anyone would fabricate all these lies about my son."

"Madeline, I know this is very difficult for you, but I do have to tell you they have proof on a tape recording of Jordan. I would like to have Julianne, Jake, and both of us sit down to discuss this before we even bring Jordan or Kylie into it."

"Absolutely not. I will confront Jordan and Kylie myself. I knew this girl being brought into our family was going to be trouble. If Conrad were still alive, I'd kill him myself for putting us in this mess." Madeline stood and started to leave without another word.

"That would be a huge mistake, Madeline. I can assure you that Jordan is out of control. He had my receptionist, Erin, on his payroll. We suspect she was spying on Conrad's business with me for years and now on Julianne's affairs. We believe he went to Singapore after Erin told him she heard about Julianne and her mother. Madeline, he threatened her mother when she was on her deathbed. How heartless and cold does a person have to be to do that?"

Madeline turned back to Christopher with fury in her eyes, but didn't respond. She walked out, slamming the door.

A Stranger in the Will

FORTY-SIX

Madeline was seething as she walked to her car, not knowing how she would approach her children tonight, but she knew she had to.

Suddenly, she put the car in park and looked up, realizing she was staring at the entrance to Simms Trading. *What on earth? How did I get here?* she thought. Try as she might to take her foot of the brake and turn to go home, she couldn't. She sat there for quite some time before deciding to speak with Jordan now.

"Mrs. Simms, how nice to see you." The guard smiled as Madeline passed him by without acknowledging his greeting. As the door closed on the elevator, she spotted her reflection looking back at her. Her anger was very apparent in her eyes and the set of her jaw. *My son*, she thought, *what have you done?*

Jordan was startled as his mother pushed open his office door without knocking.

"Mother, what are you doing here? What's the matter?"

"Jordan, tell me what I'm hearing isn't true." Tears were starting to gather in her eyes.

Jordan went to his mother's side to help her sit in one of the chairs facing his desk. He felt her shaking as he held on to her.

"Mother, you have to tell me what you've heard before I can tell you if it's true or not." Jordan was starting to feel this was not going to be good.

Madeline took a tissue out of her purse, starting to dab at her eyes. "I just came from Christopher Romano's office. He showed me a list of things."

"What things?" Starting to relax, Jordan thought this was something to do with his father's estate.

She handed him the copy of the list the attorney had given her. "These things, Jordan, these very disturbing things. Did you do any of them?" Suddenly, there was no question, she could tell by the look on his face as he continued to read that his guilt could not be denied.

He looked from the list to his mother. "Who gave this to Christopher? Why did he call you instead of me?" he yelled in anger as he slapped the list against his mother's shoulder.

"Jordan, don't you hit me again, ever! Your actions right now are telling me you did those things. Tell me I'm wrong, Jordan, please!"

"Shut up, Mother, I can't think!"

Madeline jumped up from her chair. "Jordan Simms, don't you speak to me that way. I want to know what you've done and if your sister is involved as well."

Jordan faced his mother and, as the hatred in his eyes registered, she realized he was out of control. For the first time in her life, she was frightened of her own son.

"Jordan, I'm leaving. I am calling Christopher to make an appointment for all of us to discuss those accusations against you. If you have done those things, Jordan, you could lose everything your father left you. What were you thinking?"

"Mother, sit back down."

"No, I won't sit back down. I'm leaving." Madeline started toward the door.

Jordan made it to the door before his mother, and he slammed and locked it.

"Jordan, get out of my way!" she yelled.

"Mother, I said sit down." Jordan took her by the arm and forcibly pushed her back into the chair. "Now that you've opened a door into my life that you can't close, you're going to do as I say and pretend this meeting never happened. You tell Christopher Romano that you spoke to me and that I assured you the accusations were false. I will call him and take it from there. Do you understand, Mother?" Madeline was only able to stare at him. "Do you?" he yelled.

"Yes, but..."

"No but, Mother. You forget all of this, or I swear you'll regret it."

Jordan opened the door, helped his mother out of the chair, and ushered her out of his office. He closed the door behind her, leaving her in the hallway, shaking.

Madeline managed to make it on her own to the ladies room, where she freshened up and, redid enough of her makeup to get her out the door without any questions.

FORTY-SEVEN

Neither Jake nor Julianne had heard from Christopher Romano, prompting Jake to place a call. Romano picked up immediately as the call was put through.

"Good afternoon, Jake. What can I do for you?"

"Mr. Romano, Julianne and I were just talking about our list and wondered if you had a chance to talk to Mrs. Simms yet. It's been a couple of days since we met with you."

"Yes, Jake, I met with her the next day. It didn't go really well, she didn't believe any of it and planned on talking to Jordan herself."

"Oh boy," Jake said, "that probably isn't a good idea."

"I didn't think so either, but as it turns out, Jordan is meeting with me at two o'clock today. Says his mother said some things about a list. He doesn't understand what she was going on about so he would like to have a chat with me about it."

"After you talk with him, would you call us?"

"Jake, you do know that, with confidentiality and such, I won't be able to tell you much. What I would like to do is set up a meeting with you, Julianne, Jordan and myself, if he'll agree. I'll let you know if that's going to happen."

"Okay, we'll be waiting for your call, and thank you again for your help."

As Jake hung up, he explained to Julianne what was going on.

"So we wait," he said.

"I'll never be able to go back to Simms Trading once Jordan saw that list. You know that don't you? There goes my chance at making a career out of that." Julianne was honestly disappointed.

"I know," Jake said. "Maybe I'll have to train you to be a P.I., and we'll start a partnership." They both laughed.

FOURTY-EIGHT

Jordan arrived at Christopher Romano's office precisely at two o'clock. With niceties out of the way, Jordan got right down to business.

"Christopher, I want to know what's with this list I got from my mother? Where the hell did it come from? I want to know who is accusing me of this crap."

"They are very serious accusations, Jordan. Of course you have a right to know where they came from. Sit down and we'll discuss it."

"I don't want to sit down, Christopher, and, for your information, I'm sure I can guess who told you all this."

"Jordan, is there any truth to it?"

"Well, basically, yeah." Jordan didn't care who knew anymore. He truly was out of control.

Romano opened his mouth, but the words would not come out. He was honestly speechless.

Finally, he gathered his thoughts. "Jordan, what do you think you're going to accomplish doing these things, outside of ending up behind bars for the rest of your life? As much as your father knew you could be a problem, I'm sure even he didn't anticipate you going this far. Is Kylie involved in all this as well?"

"Kylie, Kylie, Kylie. You and my Mother are so concerned about Kylie. Yes, she knew I was up to something, but she didn't know exactly what. She's so stupid, a moron could have figured it out knowing as much as she did."

"How much is that, Jordan?"

"Christopher, don't concern yourself anymore with Kylie. Now, I know Julianne and her P.I. made up this list because only they would know all of this. So, what are we going to do about them?"

"Not what you have in mind, I'm sure," Christopher said. "Jordan, you need to go to the police and turn yourself in. You need help. They'll probably send you for treatment, not lock you up."

"They're not sending me anywhere because I'm not going anywhere."

Jordan produced a gun from his jacket pocket and waived it at Christopher.

"Whoa, Jordan, what the hell are you doing? Why don't you just give that to me, and we'll forget you ever did this."

"No, Christopher, I can't do that. I will tell you what I told my mother. You have invaded my life, and there's no turning back."

"What have you done to your mother, Jordan?"

"Nothing. She'll never say anything, I'm her precious son after all. However, I'm not so sure about you."

"Jordan, I assure you I can't say anything, I am bound by attorney/client privilege. I can't tell anyone anything."

"Then why should I turn myself in if nobody can or will say anything? Somehow that doesn't make any sense, Christopher."

"Jordan, I can help you. You must realize you need it."

"No, I don't realize any such thing. I'm exercising my right to protect what's mine. I am allowed by law to do that, am I not?"

"Not by killing people just because they're in your way, no!"

"Enough! Get up, Christopher. We're going for a little ride," Jordan said, with the gun still pointed at Romano.

Romano held his hands up, crossing his arms to form an 'X' across his chest. "Jordan, put that down. There is no reason for you to do this."

"But there will be if you don't get up. Now!"

Right then, the office door opened. Jordan was still facing the attorney, so he quickly stashed the gun back in his jacket, while sending Romano a look of warning.

"Oh, I'm sorry Christopher," said Tom, one of the fellow attorneys. "The temp at the front desk said you didn't have anyone in here with you. I'll come back. My apologies to you and your client."

The intrusion offered Christopher the opportunity to give Jordan a reason to leave without him.

"It's all right, Tom, I'll only be a few more minutes. When we're done here, I'll come to your office."

Tom just nodded in agreement and closed the door.

A Stranger in the Will

"Very shrewd, Christopher. Good save for now, but don't think for a minute that we're done with this." Jordan turned and stormed out.

Romano sat back in his chair and let out a huge sigh. While wiping beads of sweat off his forehead with trembling hands, he knew too well that his associate Tom had possibly just saved his life.

FOURTY-NINE

Jake was getting nervous and pacing, wondering why Christopher Romano had not called back. It was five o'clock, and he was concerned about the outcome of the meeting, knowing Jordan was capable of anything when provoked.

"He may have had other clients after Jordan," Julianne remarked.

Jake agreed, but he didn't like it and was truly concerned. He knew Jordan would be furious that he and Julianne had gone to the attorney, and he was right.

Meanwhile, all the way home Jordan was thinking about his next move. *This was not ending here*, he thought. He placed a call to Blake.

"Blake, where are you?"

"I'm at the gas station. What's up?"

"Meet me at my office in fifteen minutes." He spun around to head back. It was the only place he felt in complete control.

Jordan instructed Blake not to check in with the guards, but to enter the building through the maintenance entrance. It had occurred to him that the fewer people who witnessed her going in and out of his office, the better.

"Hey, Jordan, where's the fire?" Blake said as she entered his office. She could tell immediately he was in no mood for her attempt at humor. She sat in her usual chair in front of his desk and waited for him to say something.

"What have you been doing, Blake? I've been waiting to hear something about your plan to take care of Jake Matthews. Instead I get handed a damning list of accusations against me from my mother, given to my attorney by Jake and Julianne. Why haven't you taken care of him yet?"

Blake was taken by surprise, "Jordan, I felt it was a bit soon since Ivan and the failed hit at Jake's house. I don't want to put myself out there like that, it's too risky."

"I don't give a crap. I pay you a lot of money to take those risks, Blake. I want it done now. If he's out of the picture, this list will go away. I don't think Julianne will pursue it any longer on her own."

"I'll set it up in the next couple of days. Just watch the news."

"Good. See that it's as clean as Ivan was, and you won't get caught. Now get out of here."

Blake left Jordan's office hating him more than she did before she went in. On her way down the elevator she was thinking, *If I didn't need the money from the second half of this contract, you'd be next Jordan.*

FIFTY

When Blake arrived home she began putting a plan together. "Okay, Mr. P.I., get ready 'cause this time I won't miss.

She spent some time going through her arsenal, selecting which piece she would use. She cleaned her Glock 9mm and gathered all she would need to do the job. The next morning she placed a call.

"Jake Matthews Investigation Services, how can I help you?" Julianne answered.

"Yes, good morning. I am in need of a private investigator. I found Mr. Matthews in the telephone book and wondered if he was accepting new clients and how long I'd have to wait to get an appointment."

"Yes, he is taking new clients. Can you hold for a moment?"

"Sure, thank you," Blake replied.

Julianne returned to the caller, informing her that Jake had a couple of hours free at three o'clock today, if that would work for her.

"Yes, that would be wonderful, thank you so much.

Julianne wrote the potential clients name, Carol Blye, in that time slot on the desk calendar. "Okay, Miss Blye, we'll see you at three."

"You bet," Blake replied with a smirk.

A Stranger in the Will

Blake tucked her long black hair under the blonde wig she had chosen and secured it. Next she chose blue tinted contact lenses, large sunglasses, and a form fitting, low cut, blood red, spaghetti strap, leather jumpsuit. She finished off with black stilettos and a lightweight black cardigan. *There now, that ought to distract him.*

After she finished dressing, she checked herself in the full length mirror behind her bedroom door. *Wow!* She thought, *when she saw what was staring back at her. What man could resist this? Distraction accomplished.*

As she stood staring at herself, she remembered what a handsome, well built man Jake Matthews is. She knew she couldn't allow him much reaction time, considering his size and strength, he could be a real danger for her. *Such a shame,* she thought, *what a waste of a perfect male specimen.*

Blake went to the phone to call Jordan as a heads-up that she was on her way to an appointment with Jake. It would be done within the hour.

"Okay, Blake, keep it clean and simple. Don't you touch Julianne, under any circumstances. Do you understand me?"

"Yes," Blake answered, with unmistakable anger. She decided right then that Jordan definitely would be next. *That pompous ass has scolded me like a child for the last time.* Then she headed for her car.

FIFTY-ONE

It was 2:45 p.m. when Blake entered Jake's office. Julianne heard the door and came out to greet her.

"Ms. Blye?" Julianne questioned.

"Yes," Blake replied.

"Please follow me." Julianne motioned as she escorted her to Jake's office.

Jake stood and extended his hand in greeting as Julianne exited, closing the door behind her.

"Miss Blye, please have a seat and tell me how I can help you."

Blake's appearance held him captive for a few seconds. Jake thought she was a beautiful woman. By the look he gave her, Blake knew she had his full attention. Now was the time to make her move.

She slowly removed the Glock from the large bag she was carrying. Bringing it up above desk level she pointed it at Jake and told him to stay quiet.

"You and the lady out front have been very busy causing problems for the wrong people, Mr. Matthews. I'm only sorry I missed the first time and gave you time to do more damage. That has caused huge problems with my employer."

"Blake, I presume?" Jake said as he placed his clasped hands on the desk and leaned forward.

A Stranger in the Will

"Ah, Ivan told you. I was in the trees that day, you know. I was watching you hunting for me. It was quite entertaining actually."

While Blake was busy verbally patting herself on the back, Jake heard the door and his friend Nick's voice in the front office. He had to make a choice. Should he move to prevent any major damage or lunge at her? He didn't have time to do either. Blake aimed and fired. Luckily the bullet only hit his shoulder. Jake ducked behind his desk to grab his own gun as Nick came through the office door. With his gun drawn, he dropped to his knees as Blake spun around. Nick fired, and Blake fell forward off the chair onto the floor. Nick could see her eyes wide with surprise and knew she was gone.

Nick called out for Jake as he saw him rise above the desk, his bloodied hand holding his shoulder.

"I'm okay, it's just a graze." He walked around the corner of the desk where Blake had fallen. Seeing her gun lying next to her, he realized it could have turned out much worse.

"Thanks buddy. Good timing."

"Saving your hide is getting to be a habit, my friend." Nick grinned.

Julianne hung up from calling the police and ran into Jake's office, gasping as she noticed Jake had been shot.

"I'm okay, it's not as bad as it looks," Jake assured her as he reached out for her hand.

The police and ambulance arrived quickly. The police took statements, while the EMT's tended to

Jake's shoulder. When the coroner arrived, she did a preliminary check and her findings supported the statements given, so the scene was cleared.

Jake, Nick, and Julianne's statements all told the whole story of Ivan and Blake and their "working relationship" with Jordan Simms. The officers looked perplexed at the mention of Jordan Simms being involved in a murder plot. Jake told them to look up the two statements he previously made at the police station, that no one had believed.

A Stranger in the Will

FIFTY-TWO

At five o'clock, Jordan was nervously twitching, sitting at his desk waiting to hear from Blake. Knowing she should have been done an hour ago, he turned on his office TV. ...Breaking News,...he saw printed across the screen. His heartbeat picked up as he leaned back in his chair to enjoy the story. The reporter was standing outside Jake's office building. Jordan's smile grew bigger.

The reporter began to broadcast:

"I am standing in front of the building that houses 'Jake Matthews Investigation Services'. An unidentified woman, only known as Blake, has just been shot and killed by an off duty police officer yet to be identified. The only information we have been given so far is that the deceased is a white female, suspected to be between 25 to 30 years old. She used the fake name Carol Blye to book an appointment with Jake Matthews, the owner of Jake Matthews Investigation Services. The victim apparently had a score to settle with Mr. Matthews. The agency secretary, Julianne Sullivan told us that Blake made the appointment this morning. She arrived about 2:45 p.m. and was escorted into Mr. Matthew's office. Miss Sullivan said she heard a gunshot shortly after returning to her desk. The police have since taken

Ms. Sullivan back inside, so unfortunately, that's all the information I have been able to obtain for now. Back to the station.

Jordan began banging his fists on his desk, the sounds vibrating off the walls of his office. The banging and accompanying language could be heard out in the hallway. Kylie was just about to knock, but hearing all that, she thought better of it and headed back to her office.

Jordan stood and started to panic. His mind going at warp speed trying to think of what he should do next. *Obviously,* he thought, *I have to do this myself.*

He picked up the phone and dialed Jake's business number.

The answering machine picked up. After Julianne's recorded greeting and at the tone, he started to speak.

"Julianne, this is Jordan. I just saw the news. Are you and Jake okay? If you need anything, call me. This is horrible news, but perhaps now that the threat to the two of you is over, you can come back and pursue your career at Simms Trading. Call me when you get a chance, and we'll discuss that."

When he hung up, he was already plotting how to get rid of Julianne Sullivan. Jake Matthews would just be a bonus.

A Stranger in the Will

FIFTY-THREE

After everyone left, Julianne straightened up the office and locked up, while Jake and Nick went to the office for a chat.

Julianne went upstairs to try and calm herself. Still shaking, she poured herself a glass of wine and sat on the sofa, staring into space. Jake came in and startled her. She held her hand over her heart in panic.

"Are you okay?" he asked as he wrapped her in his arms. "I'm so sorry, I didn't mean to scare you. I didn't realize you were so deep in thought."

"Jake, that was way too close. It's much too easy for someone to get to us. I was thinking, maybe I should move back to Singapore. You could come too and open up an investigation business there. Jordan would have to spend a lot more to have someone track us and get there once they found us. I thought about Denver as well, but that's not far enough out of his reach."

"Julianne, I am not by any means saying that is out of the question, but do you have any idea how wealthy Jordan is? Money would not even enter into his plans or what he chooses to do. While I would have no objection to living in Singapore, I have to believe that's the first place he'd look.

"Of course, Jake, you're right. I didn't think it through very well. It's just that I'm scared, and not only for me, but obviously you too." she said while pointing to his bandaged arm.

"I know, baby. I agree with your reasoning, but we need to find a way to put Jordan Simms away for good."

Just as he finished, his eye caught the blinking from the alert he installed on his apartment phone, he saw they had a message on the office phone. They went to the office, pushed the button, and heard Jordan's voice. They listened in complete amazement as he began his message. When the message was done, they both just stared, speechless due to Jordan's audacity.

"Oh my Lord, Jake, he's not going to stop until one or both of us is dead."

They reached out to each other. Silently, they stood in an embrace meant to comfort, but it fell short of that objective.

Julianne was the first to break away. "Jake, let's go out somewhere and have a nice relaxing dinner where we can get away from here for awhile. I can't stay here right now."

Jake looked down at his bloodstained clothes. "Okay, I'll take a quick shower, change, and we'll be on our way."

Julianne nodded and headed to her room to freshen up.

A Stranger in the Will

FIFTY-FOUR

As they entered Olive Garden, Julianne thanked Jake for agreeing to her choice for dinner. She immediately started to relax as she smelled the salad, bread sticks, and Chicken Alfredo.

"Just think, we can ask for a corner table, have some wine, a good meal, and spend some time alone without any fear. How great does that sound?"

"Fantastic," Jake replied.

As they both relaxed, Jake was determined to keep the conversation away from Jordan and what was going on.

"Tell me what Singapore is like, I'd really like to see it someday. And how do you like L.A.? Taking out all the bad stuff, of course."

Julianne proceeded to tell him all about her life in Singapore, including the promise she broke to her mother.

"Outside of what's been happening since I started all this, L.A. is a great place. Lots going on and lots to do. The best part has been meeting all of you. Donna is a lovely person, and Nick! Jake, you couldn't ask for a better friend." She looked Jake right in the eyes with that sassy little attitude of hers. She knew he was waiting to hear what she had to say about him. "Jake, I am so glad that I asked your aunt, in the library, if she knew anything of the P.I's I had written down."

Jake interrupted her. "Yeah, her commission is getting bigger all the time," he smiled.

Julianne smiled back with the twinkle in her eyes that tore at his very being.

"I guess I'll have to split that commission with you. I owe her big time as well. I've never met anyone that is as kind and compassionate as you are. I wouldn't have thought someone in your line of business would be a sensitive sort with all the things you see going on. You are truly a wonderful person, Jake Matthews." She took his hands. "And, like it or not, I'm afraid I've fallen in love with you."

Jake about fell off his chair. He thought so and hoped so, but he wasn't sure. With a sparkle in his eyes and the goofy grin he had on his face she thought was priceless, he said, "Damn girl! It took you long enough to say it. I was having a heart attack over here." They both laughed out loud, then looked around kind of embarrassed.

"Julianne? You have to know I love you. I think I knew I was in for the long haul the first time I saw you."

"I knew you did, but not quite that long ago," she said.

"Let's go home," Jake said.

A Stranger in the Will

FIFTY-FIVE

Driving down the road to home, Jake noticed a car sitting in the dark, all the way at the other end of the road. Although the car was far enough away to not be a threat to them, Jake still took note because that same car was there when they left. He wasn't alarmed, due to there being a few businesses at that end of the road, but he was concerned enough to be cautious in light of all that had been going on.

When they got inside, Jake locked up and followed Julianne upstairs. He tried to search the house without her knowing. When he was satisfied, he went downstairs, searched there, got his gun, and went outside. The car was gone. He scolded himself that he was getting paranoid and, went back inside.

After seeing Jake's car return home, Jordan left. He stopped and got something to eat on his way home. Now he knew for certain where Jake lived and that Julianne was staying with him. He was trying to put a plan together as to how he was going to eliminate Jake first so he wouldn't interfere with his plans for his lovely half sister.

Jake and Julianne settled on the sofa to watch the news and then headed off to bed. Both knew that tonight would be a night to remember after each of them opened up about their feelings.

Julianne took a shower and climbed into bed. Jake had anticipation nipping at him while he took another shower. Anxious to hold her and make love to her after all this time was more than he could stand. When he finished his shower he opened the bathroom door, only to find her lying there sound asleep. As much as he wanted her, he couldn't wake her. He put his bathrobe on and went to the living room to watch a movie, hoping that would alleviate his disappointment.

Jake managed to grab the phone as soon as it started to ring.

"Hey, Jake, how's it going?" Nick asked. "I was by earlier, but you guys were gone. Everything okay?"

"Yeah, Julianne wanted to get out of here for awhile, so we went to dinner."

"That was probably a good idea. Did it help?" Nick asked.

"Yes, it did. We both relaxed and talked about us, for a change. It was very nice, we both shared our feelings, and that turned out great," Jake commented.

"I'm happy for you both, you make a nice couple. It's about time you found someone, Jake."

"Yes, it is. I just hope I can stop Jordan Simms before he does something. Which brings me to a question. When you were here did you happen to notice a car parked all the way down at the end of the street?"

"No, but there was a car pulling a u-turn in your parking lot. Looked like a pretty expensive one. I didn't pay a lot of attention to it, so I'm not sure what kind. Why do you ask?"

"There was a car parked at the end when we left and still there when we came home. I went out a few minutes later, and it was gone. Just being a bit on edge, I guess."

"I'm on graveyard tonight. I'll make some passes by your place while I'm out so you can rest easy, my friend"

"Thanks, buddy. I'll check in with you tomorrow."

FIFTY-SIX

Julianne woke up alone in bed. She glanced toward the bathroom, but no Jake. She quickly threw her bathrobe on and went looking for him. She found him asleep on the sofa with the TV still going. Getting on her knees she leaned over and kissed him, whispering in his ear how sorry she was that she fell asleep while he was in the shower. When she went to stand up, Jake grabbed her hand and pulled her on top of him.

Their playful moment was interrupted as Jake's phone began to ring, and it rang and rang until he heard Nick's voice on the answering machine. "Pick up, Jake," the urgency in his voice telling Jake he had better get it.
"Nick, what's wrong?"
"I'm outside, you had better come out, now!"
"I'll be right there."
Julianne had picked up enough of the conversation to know something wasn't right, so she got up and asked Jake what was wrong?
"Nick's outside, and he said I should get out there now."
They both scrambled to quickly get dressed and went downstairs.
As Jake opened the door he saw Nick standing there, holding a picture of Christopher Romano with a knife held to his throat, but not showing

A Stranger in the Will

who was holding it. It didn't take a lot of street smarts to figure it out.

"Where did you get that?"

"I was making my final ride-by for my shift and found it taped to your door."

"Jake, there's a note written on the back. You better read it."

The note read:

Jake, I don't believe I need to tell you who is holding this knife. Mr. Romano is still breathing, but I won't guarantee how long. That will depend on how soon you can get here to save him. There's an empty warehouse on 72nd St. It's the only building about a mile beyond the strip mall. I suggest you come alone and hurry. You've got a half an hour, and the clock is ticking.

"Jake, you can't go there alone," Julianne cried as she looked around. "How can he give you a half an hour, he has to be watching us to know when you got the note." Jake's hair prickled on the back of his neck as he turned and rushed Julianne back in the house.

"He's not going alone," Nick said as he followed.

Jordan snickered to himself as he watched them scurry into the house, then he left. On the way back to the warehouse, he was getting concerned that Jake's cop friend would be joining them, and that didn't thrill him. *Maybe I should have just taken them out while they were standing out in the open*, he thought. *But then I would miss out on the thrill of the chase.*

"Jake, I can't show up in my squad car, so I have to go back to the station, clock out, and get my car. I'll meet you at the strip mall, we'll make a plan of attack, and I'll stay out of sight until it's time."

"I'll get what I think we'll need and head over. We should be there within 5 minutes of each other," Jake replied.
Nick nodded, jumped in his car, and sped off.

"Jake, you have to call the police!" Julianne yelled.

Jake took her by the arms to face him. "If I do that, Christopher will die. Jordan may also, or he may get away. I can't take that chance.

I want you to pack up a few things and go to a hotel for a couple of days. If Jordan should win this battle, he'll come right for you. Don't leave any clues here as to where you are going. I'll call your cell phone."

"But Jake..."

"Honey, I'm sorry, but it has to be this way. So please, go call a cab, pack some of your things, and get out of here for now. Please Julianne."

She hugged him and turned to go pack and call her cab.

Jake gathered up everything he could think of that he and Nick might need. It was time to go. He left without another good-bye to Julianne. He hoped he would never regret that.

A Stranger in the Will

FIFTY-SEVEN

Both men pulled into the strip mall at the same time. Twenty minutes of the half hour Jake was given had already passed.

"Nick, we can't take both cars, he'll see. Why don't you lie down on the backseat? I doubt Jordan will leave Christopher to come out and check the car."

"I agree," Nick said.

They took a couple of minutes to discuss their plan, put their vests on, and head to the abandoned warehouse.

As they approached the building Jake said he could see a truck parked along the side, and that was the only vehicle visible.

"Okay," Jake said, "here we go."

"I'm right behind you," Nick replied

Jake got out of the car and stood there for a few minutes, checking out the area. As he started to walk away from the car, a shot rang out, missing him by only inches. He dropped to the ground and whispered to Nick, "That came from the woods along-side the warehouse."

Then he heard Jordan. "Sorry Jake, you're too late. The attorney is already dead. You and my illegitimate sister shouldn't have involved him to begin with, and she shouldn't have gotten you involved. Now you have to die before I can be free to grab her without your interference."

"Why don't you come out and fight like a man? Winner gets Julianne. You're a coward to hide behind the trees and take your potshots, Jordan," Jake said

"I'm not a fool, Jake. I know I am not physically equal to you, so I think we'll just keep things this way. You come and find me. I have no doubt you have a gun on you. That will keep things even."

Jake was trying to keep Jordan talking so he could get an idea of Jordan's location and Nick could open the back door just enough to squeeze out without being heard.

"Okay, I think I have his location within a few feet," Jake whispered to his partner as he pointed in that direction. Both gave thumbs up as they separated.

Jake appeared from behind the car doing a zigzag run, hoping to distract Jordan from Nick running around to the back of Jordan's approximate position. As Jake reached the tree line, he saw Nick do the same.

"Jordan, it doesn't seem your shooting skills are any better than your ability to fight."

"I was just practicing, Jake. I want you much closer when I kill you so that I can see your face at the moment you realize I'm going to have Julianne to myself."

Jake felt the hair on the back of his neck stand straight up at the thought.

A Stranger in the Will

Jordan was sneaking very quietly toward the sound of Jake's voice as he was chiding him, and Nick was doing the same to Jordan.

Jordan heard a twig crack behind him. He stopped and turned toward the noise. He thought he saw a shadow. He veered off his course a bit. "Jake, we have company. Is he with you? That wasn't the deal."

That was the last they heard from Jordan. He had previously made himself very familiar with the wooded area just in case, and he was gone.

Jake and Nick went inside the warehouse to find Romano. He wasn't there. They checked the truck along the side of the warehouse, but found nothing. It was all a set-up.

FIFTY-EIGHT

With Jordan on the run, Jake called Julianne to make sure she had left the house already.

"Hello, Jake," she answered. "Are you guys okay? Did you get Jordan?"

Jake could hear the tension in her voice. "Yes, we're fine honey, but Jordan got away through the woods. I wanted to call to make sure you were safely out of the house."

"I checked into the Beverly Wilshire. They have the best security and privacy practices for their guests. I'm in room 201."

"Okay, good choice. I'll be over as soon as I can."

"Jake, what about Christopher? Did you find him?"

"No, we didn't, nor any evidence that he was even here.

"Oh Jake, if Jordan did kill him, how will you ever find him? He shouldn't be left out there alone."

"I know, Julianne. We'll find him."

Meanwhile, Jordan rushed home, packed what he felt he would need, and went into hiding. He would get to Jake Matthews in due time.

Later the next morning Jake called the attorney's office, but they had not heard from him or seen him all day. They also informed Jake that the attorney missed two appointments this morning.

A Stranger in the Will

Jake removed the picture from his pocket. He and Nick studied it carefully in hopes of a clue as to where it was taken. The background was plain white. It was no help.

On the way to the hotel, Jake stopped by Romano's office, hoping someone would give him the attorney's home address. It took a lot of explaining and some very good side stepping of the facts, but he finally, although somewhat reluctantly, got the address from Romano's assistant.

He called Nick to make arrangements for them to meet at the address he was given. Then he placed another call to Julianne to let her know what he and Nick were about to do.

FIFTY-NINE

Jake pulled in behind Nick's car. Both men got out and leaned against it, looking at the house and, wondering how they would gain entry, legally.

Nick suggested they do a perimeter check first. "If we spot anything suspicious or see anything through the windows, we call for police back up to go in."

They both noticed the blood on the doorknob at the back of the house. "I think we found Christopher," Jake said.

"I hope not," Nick replied. "Maybe there's another reason for the blood." He was trying to be optimistic. "I'll get the police out here."

After Nick left, Jake knocked on the door, desperately hoping that Romano would come to answer.

Nick came back around and told Jake the police were on their way.

As they walked back around the front to wait, Jake told Nick about knocking on the door to see if Romano was in there. "I thought that, if he was injured, he would at least know someone was out here if he was able to yell for help."

"Not a bad idea," Nick replied.

They leaned against Jake's car again and, could hear the sirens off in the distance. The call Nick made as a possible homicide had solicited the quick response he hoped for. They pushed off the car as the two squad cars pulled up. Nick knew both officers personally, so, as they shook hands, he introduced Jake.

Brian had 20 years on the force, and he was the first to speak. "Well, shall we?" Brian said, as he motioned toward the house. They all fell in behind him when he took the lead.
"Who is the homeowner?" he asked Nick.
Nick explained who Romano was and why they had suspicions as to his fate inside that house. Again, eyebrows went up at the mention of Jordan Simms being involved in what could be waiting for them when they entered.
The smell inside as they opened the door told them immediately what they wanted to know. With something covering their faces, they spread out in search of the source.
Jake yelled from the kitchen. They all headed there, knowing in the pit of their stomachs what Jake had found. He stood over the body, which he identified to the officers as that of Attorney Christopher Romano. The attorney had indeed died as Jordan had insinuated he would. Jake then took the picture out of his pocket and handed it to Brian, explaining it was found taped to the door of his office. The white wall in the picture they had wondered about earlier was behind Romano's body. The kitchen table had been pulled away from the wall to create the backdrop.
Brian placed the call to summon the coroner and the forensics team. The coroner confirmed that

time of death was about 24 hours ago. Nick and Jake looked at each other, their nods confirming that would be about right. Statements were taken and they were free to go.

An APB was put out for Jordan Simms. Too many coincidences had built up for the authorities to continue to deny Jordan Simms's involvement.

Meanwhile, Jordan was holed up in a motel much below his standards, trying to lie low for a few days while planning his next move. He knew he had to get rid of Jake next, but the question was how.

A Stranger in the Will

SIXTY

Jake went to his office again before going to the Beverly Wilshire. As he drove into his parking lot, he noticed a car he didn't recognize. Pulling over a little farther from the office than usual, he cut the engine and quietly got out. He drew his gun and slowly approached the building. As he was trying to see through the windows, he scolded himself for not washing them more often. Then he saw movement. With his gun at the ready, he slowly turned the doorknob, again chastising himself for forgetting to set the alarm before they went on the hunt for Jordan. As he was swinging the door open with a quick jolt, Donna whipped around, screaming.

"Donna!" He yelled louder than he intended to, as he holstered his gun.

"Oh Jake, you scared me!" She immediately walked into his arms, tears streaking her cheeks.

Inching her away, he said. "Donna, what are you doing here? You look great, by the way. All better?"

"Yes, everything is fine. The doctor says I can resume normal activity."

"Honey, that is the best thing I've heard since this all started. I'm sorry I scared you, but I didn't recognize the car."

"It's just a rental, we sold our cars. That's what I came to talk to you about. I was leaving a note for you to call me."

"Sounds mysterious. What's going on?"

"You know Brad and I took a trip to the islands with the money Ivan gave us." Jake nodded his head. "Well, we fell in love with St. Croix, and we've decided to move there." She held Jake's gaze as if looking for his approval.

Jake walked with her over to the client seating area so they could sit to talk about what was devastating news to him. "Donna, of course I am very happy for you and Brad. After what you've been though it's great to see that twinkle back in your eyes. For selfish reasons I don't like that you're leaving to go so far away, but I am thrilled if it will make both of you happy. When are you planning this adventure?"

They continued to talk about plans, Jake's future, and Julianne's role in it. They talked about the on-going Jordan drama and the effect it's having on the agency.

Then, Donna stood to finish gathering her things from her desk. They hugged, Donna cried, and Jake got a bit melancholy. They said their good-byes, and she left.

As Jake watched her walk away he felt an emptiness in himself... Donna had been with him for so long. He felt he was losing a piece of himself as his heart filled with sadness.

Jake's cell rang, Julianne was just wondering if he was okay. He assured her he was and that he was on his way.

A Stranger in the Will

"What's wrong, Jake? You sound, I don't know, sad."

"I'll be there shortly and will explain everything. It's been a hell of a day."

"Okay, I'll see you in a few minutes. Be careful."

"It's 3:45 p.m. now, but I should be there by 4:30."

SIXTY-ONE

Jake went through the day's mail and phone messages. He straightened his desk and headed for his door.

Jake heard the outside door open and called out, but, no one answered. The hair on the back of his neck immediately reacted, once again. He walked to the wall dividing his office from reception.

Backing up against it, he drew his gun while sliding across to the entryway.

"Hello?" he said, but still no answer. Something in his gut told him it was Jordan. Jake could picture Jordan standing at the ready for him to come out. He knew he wouldn't stand a chance.

Jake decided his best chance for survival would be lying on his stomach and looking into the reception area from the floor. Whoever the intruder might be would be looking about midway up the door frame for someone to peek out. So, he chose the floor method and, sure enough, it was Jordan Simms with a gun pointed right at mid door. Jake stood and put some distance between the wall and himself. He was well aware the wall would not offer any protection from a bullet.

"Jordan," Jake said, "we found Christopher Romano. You didn't have to do that, Jordan. He was bound by attorney/client privilege, so he couldn't have hurt you."

"Well, better be safe than sorry, I always say. Where's your cop buddy, Jake? Anywhere around here?"

"No, it's just us, Jordan, so why don't you tell me why you're here?"

"Oh, come on, Jake, you're not that stupid, but I shall enlighten you anyway. I want you dead and out of my hair. You've been a real pain in the ass, you know. I want Julianne. I'm sure you know I am not going to allow her to interfere with Simms Trading. My father had no right to give her the power he did."

"Come on, Jordan, Kylie was given the same thing. Are you going to kill her too?"

"Kylie will not buck the system. She will do as I tell her. Don't you worry about her."

"Jordan, you can't believe you are going to walk right back to your fancy office like nothing happened. The police are already looking for you for Romano's murder."

"Ah hell, Jake, you think being an upstanding citizen in this community I can't talk my way out of that? There is no proof! I left no evidence, and I do not intend to leave you in any better shape than the poor attorney. I'm sorry, Jake, but you won't be the one to point a finger at me anymore."

Jake had turned his recorder on when he pushed himself away from the wall. He smiled to himself, knowing Jordan was putting a noose around his own neck with every word he spoke.

Jordan spun around as the office door opened.

"Ah, Julianne, Jake and I were just discussing how this mess you created was going to end. How convenient of you to join us and make it so much easier for me."

"Julianne!" Jake yelled. "What are you doing? Why did you leave the hotel?"

Julianne, realizing what was happening, had to think fast. "Jordan, I was looking for you, actually. I wanted to tell you that I would love to continue to work for Simms Trading. It's kind of a way for me to get to know what kind of man my father was. I am willing to sign off on my appointment as a controlling partner. You can keep the business all to yourself, if all this nonsense will just stop. I want all this drama and killing to be over." She was thinking all of that would satisfy Jordan so he would leave.

Jake stood in his office, dumbfound at what Julianne was saying. He eventually did understand why she was doing it.

"Julianne, do you honestly think for one minute that I could be persuaded to believe no one would ever say anything to the authorities about any of this?" Jordan demanded.

"I give you my word, Jordan. Jake, tell him you won't say anything either, and we'll sign whatever Jordan wants us to."

As Jake looked toward the tape recorder, Julianne let out a hard scream when Jordan took a handful of her hair and pulled her up against his side.

Jake snuck a quick look out his door to see what happened.

"All right, Jordan, let her go. I'm coming out." Jake walked out to the reception area with his gun tucked under his shirt and his hands held high.

"Well, well, look at the three of us here together. I've waited a long time for this moment. I paid out a lot of money to have people do this for me, but as it turns out, I did better myself."

"Jordan, you have us here together, now let her go."

"I'm sorry, Jake, but you are really not in any position to give the orders here. However, I will let her come to you so you can be together and holding hands when you die."

Again there was the sound of a car door shutting. While still holding the gun on Jake and Julianne, Jordan walked to look out the window. "Damn!" he whispered. "It's your police pal, whatever his name is. I'm taking Julianne in your office, Jake, you had better get rid of him."

SIXTY-TWO

Jake met Nick at the door. "Hey buddy, what brings you here? Did we have a meet set up that I forgot about?"

"No, I just thought I'd stop by with an update of really nothing new. We've been searching for our friend Jordan all around town, but we've found nothing so far."

At the mention of Jordan's name, Jake rolled his eyes toward his office. Pointed his index finger like a gun and mouthed Julianne. As Nick put it all together, they started talking normal again so as to not alert Jordan.

Nick was telling Jake it was too bad they couldn't find any clues, he was a slippery one, but they'd keep looking. Jake handed Nick his keys and motioned to the back door, indicating he give Jake five minutes before coming in and to come in quietly.

Nick spoke up and said, "Well, since you're not inviting me in and you have other cars out here, I guess you're busy with new clients, so I'll head out and check back with you later. I just wanted to let you know what's going on, which isn't much. Sorry to interrupt.

"No problem. We'll talk later."

Nick started his car, drove out of the parking lot, down the street about a block, and walked back to Jake's.

A Stranger in the Will

Jordan walked Julianne back to reception and released her again to go to Jake's side. "That was very good, Jake. You gave my sister a few more minutes of life. Now, I've got a few questions I need answered, and then we'll end this and I'll be on my way."

Meanwhile, Nick was trying different keys in the back door, as quietly as he could. "Bingo," he whispered as the key turned the dead bolt. The building was old, and the door started to squeak as he tried to open it.

Jordan's ears perked up. "What was that?"

"What?" Jake asked.

Jordan just stood very quiet for a minute before he was satisfied.

Jake started to sneeze to give Nick an opportunity to get inside. He grabbed a tissue off Donna's desk and wiped at his nose to sell the whole sneezing thing.

Nick finally made it in and was standing in a corner of Jake's office. He noticed the light on the recorder when he looked at Jake's desk. He smiled to himself, knowing that was a smart move on Jake's part. He had the same idea Jake had about looking out into the other room from the bottom of the door. As he peeked around, Jake saw him and breathed a sigh of relief. Jordan's back was to the office door, so there was no chance he saw Nick. However, it did give Nick a clear shot.

Jordan started to walk toward the front door so that he would have an unobstructed exit when he was finished. Jake edged himself and Julianne around a little so Nick would still have his shot.

Jordan saw a flash of light and heard something. When he realized it was a gun-shot, he turned toward Jake's office and fired back.

Jake fell to the floor, taking Julianne with him. Jordan ran out the door, firing as he went. Jake drew his gun from under his shirt and headed to the door as Nick came out from the office.

Jordan was still firing from his car window to keep them at bay until he was far enough out of range.

Both men helped Julianne up, and Jake held her until she stopped shaking.

"I am so sorry, Jake. I didn't know Jordan was here. I was just wondering where you were when you didn't show up at the hotel. What I almost caused!" she said as she started to fall. Julianne had fainted.

Jordan pulled over in a dark, wooded area. He wasn't sure if he had been hit. He got out, checked himself over, and relief covered him like a blanket when he knew he was okay. Looking at his car riddled with bullet holes startled him. He wondered how he was going to get it back to his motel looking like that. He decided to clear everything out, take the plates off, scratched the VIN number off, and walk to the motel. It was only a couple of miles, yet it would be days before anybody discovered the car in these woods.

A Stranger in the Will

SIXTY-THREE

Jordan walked along the dark road with the comfort of the heavily wooded area along-side him. He kept checking behind him and ducking into the woods every time he saw headlights. His cell phone rang as it had several times the last few days. He decided to answer it when he saw it was Kylie.

"Jordan, where have you been? Mom and I have been frantic looking for you. You haven't been home or at the office for three days.

"Kylie, shut up and listen. I'm walking down the old back road leading to the Crescent plant. You know where I mean?"

"Yes, what are you doing walking and there of all places?"

"Never mind. I'll explain when you get here. I'm almost to the Dog & Burger, pick me up behind there. And Kylie, hurry." Jordan hung up. All of the sudden he saw flashing lights coming toward him. Knowing he didn't have time to get to the cover of the woods, he dropped into the small gully next to the road. He knew where they were headed. As soon as they passed, he jumped up and ran full throttle to the Dog & Burger. Safely out back he tried the bathroom door, but it was locked. Bending over and trying to catch his breath, he jerked up when he heard police radios crackling out front. He stood frozen. He heard the clerk saying he had not seen the car they were describing.

Kylie pulled around back just as the patrol car pulled out.

"It's about time!" Jordan yelled, as he quickly slid into the back seat on his stomach. "Go!" he shouted.

"Jordan, what the hell is going on?"

"Just get out of here, Kylie, now! I'll tell you when we get to my motel room. I need to shower and catch my breath."

"Your motel? Which is where?"

Kylie parked the car in front of her brother's motel room. Jordan jumped out and let himself in, leaving Kylie outside. She opened the door and went in, just as Jordan slammed the bathroom door. She sat down at the table by the window to call her mother to tell her she was with Jordan, but that she would have to fill her in later seeing as, she didn't know anything yet.

Jordan came out of the bathroom, looking like Jordan again.

"Jordan, are you going to tell me what's going on?"

"Look, Kylie, I'm very hungry. Would you go right over there," he said, pointing to the corner of the parking lot, "to Carl's Diner and get us something to eat? Then we'll talk."

"Jordan, damn it."

"Please Kylie, here's some money."

"All right. I'll go, but when I get back there will be no more delay. You're going to tell me what you've done." Jordan nodded his head in agreement.

The minute Kylie was out the door, Jordan threw all his things into his bag, grabbed Kylie's keys off the table, ran outside, jumped into her car and sped off.

SIXTY-FOUR

Kylie noticed her car was gone as she came out of the restaurant. The cardboard tray of food dropped to the ground as she went running toward Jordan's room. She ran inside and saw the room key sitting on the table. Checking around and seeing all of his stuff was gone, she sat on the edge of the bed and cried. When she finally pulled herself together, she called her mother to come and get her.

When Madeline arrived, Kylie told her what had gone on so far and that Jordan hadn't told her anything. Kylie told her he was coming from the direction of Jake Matthews's place. Madeline was furious. "Let's go," she said. Kylie directed her to Jake's.

By the time they got there, the police had gone. Lights were out downstairs, yet still on upstairs. Kylie looked up the phone number on her phone.

Jake noticed the indicator light on his phone was blinking, telling him there was a call coming in on the business line. "Jake Matthews Investigative Services," he answered.

"Jake, this is Kylie Simms. I'm sorry to bother you at this late hour, but my mom and I are outside. We need to talk to you. If I'm right, you had a visit from Jordan tonight. We need to talk."

"I'll be right down, Kylie."

A Stranger in the Will

"What's that all about?" Julianne asked. Jake explained that Kylie and Madeline were outside and wanted to talk.

"Oh no, Jake, you think Jordan could be with them? Should we call the police first?"

Jake went to the window overlooking the parking area. He saw Kylie and Madeline getting out of the car. He looked around and didn't see any evidence that Jordan was with them, so they went downstairs to let them in.

"Come in," Jake said, as he motioned for them to enter. "We'll go upstairs where it's more comfortable."

"Thank you for seeing us, Mr. Matthews," Madeline said as Julianne led them up the stairs.

"Please call me Jake, Mrs. Simms."

"Let's all go by first names," Kylie said.

"Okay, what can I do for you ladies?" Jake asked.

"I'm not sure where to begin. We don't have any idea what is happening with Jordan or what he's done. We can only assume it is not good," Madeline said.

Jake began to tell them about the picture that was found on his back door and about the chase through the woods at the old warehouse and about finding Christopher Romano's body. He gave them a minute to digest what he had told them before he continued with what happened just hours ago.

When Jake was finished, Kylie told them about her encounter with her brother right after he'd been here.

"I don't know what to do," Madeline said. She looked at Julianne.

"Your father and I always knew Jordan was a volatile and devious person, but never would we have thought him capable of the things he's doing. I feel so foolish for not seeing it and like such a failure as a mother."

Julianne went to kneel in front of Madeline. She took her hands. As tears ran down her face, she told Madeline how sorry she was that her need to find her father had caused so much pain and death to so many people. Madeline hugged her and told her it wasn't her fault. "Jordan is damaged, I know that," she said. "He needs help, but I don't know where to find him."

Jake stepped in. "I assure you, Madeline, I will find him. All I have to do is put myself out there. I'm sure he'll come to me."

"You won't hurt him? Please don't hurt him. He just needs help."

"I promise I won't hurt him, Madeline, unless it comes down to him or me."

"Thank you, Jake. I will pay you your normal fees if you'll let me hire you to find my son."

"We'll worry about that later. Let's just concentrate on finding him for now. Both of you have to call me with anything you hear or find out. Promise me that."

The four of them said their good-byes. Jake waited for them to be safely in their car and driving away, then locked the door and went back upstairs.

A Stranger in the Will

SIXTY-FIVE

Jordan had parked Kylie's car behind a new motel. He lay on his bed exhausted and fell asleep as he was plotting his next move.

Meanwhile, Jake was busy in his office putting together a plan to start his search for Jordan as Julianne started a late dinner. He placed a call to Nick, hoping to recruit his friends help.
"Jake, everything still okay?" Nick asked.
"Yes. After the police left, something interesting happened." Jake hesitated.
Nick waited and finally spoke up. "Well, are you going to make me guess?"
"We had more company. Madeline and Kylie paid us a very interesting visit around 7:30 tonight."
"You're joking!" Nick replied. "Tell me about it. I can't think of a reason they would do that."
Jake proceeded to tell his friend that Madeline wanted to hire him to find Jordan so he could get the help he obviously needs.
"Why you, of all people?"
Jake continued to tell Nick about Kylie picking Jordan up. "Evidently he has ditched his car in the woods between here and Dog & Burger. They drove back to his motel, he sent Kylie for some food, and, while she was gone he took off in her car."

"Jake, are you sure you want to get involved in that? He's after you and Julianne, and now you're after him?"

"This may work to our advantage, Nick. He wouldn't know we are looking for him. We can put ourselves out there, but he wouldn't know we would be fully prepared for him to come for us. He could end up making this very easy."

"Famous last words. You should know more than anyone how that can backfire, Jake. Jordan is not going to just walk right up to you, out in the open."

"I know. That's where hopefully you will come into play. First, we have to find his car in the woods around here. That can go a long way as evidence to support the statements the three of us gave."

"Okay, I can get the hunt for that going when I go on shift tomorrow morning. If he ditched it and walked to meet Kylie, it can't be too far in."

"Thanks Nick, I owe you again."

The next morning Nick got right on finding Jordan's car. He and Jake spread out and found it rather quickly. It wasn't that far from Jake's or that deep into the woods. Nick called for a tow truck, and the car was towed to the police impound lot.

With that out of the way, Jake called Kylie and made the arrangements for dividing up the sections of L.A. Nick had one for his patrol area while on his shift, Kylie had her appointed area with instructions to call Jake if she spotted her car, and Jake had his area to cover, his hope being that they would spot the car today and not have to

A Stranger in the Will

repeat the process tomorrow. L.A. is a big place, so Jake tried to keep the first search in the areas Jordan would most likely stay. He couldn't imagine him staying at a motel in the inner city. However, the first day was a bust.

The three of them met with Julianne for dinner. They discussed their search criteria for tomorrow. Nick would request a different patrol area so as not to interfere with his work schedule. Jake assigned the safer of the two areas to Kylie, and he took the most questionable.

"Let's hope we hit pay dirt tomorrow, guys. We'll be running out of areas I would be comfortable sending Kylie to, and Nick, the other areas wouldn't be part of your division's patrol zones."

After they covered all they could for today, Nick had to return his squad car, and Jake, Julianne, and Kylie were heading home for the night.

Before Kylie could get in her car, her phone rang. She saw it was Jordan so she motioned to Jake to wait a minute. Julianne waited by her car as well.

"Jordan, where the hell are you with my car? That was a pretty rotten thing you did."

"I know, Kylie, and I'm sorry. You can come and get your car. I got a rental." Jordan gave Kylie the directions to his motel, and she agreed to be there within the hour.

She told Jake where Jordan was. "I'm going to pick up my mother and take her with me so she can drive her car back home. I'll meet you over there in a half hour."

"Okay, Kylie, but don't go in until I get there." Jake said. "Julianne, you go on home, and I'll call you when this is done."

Julianne agreed, but Jake could tell she wasn't comfortable with it.

A Stranger in the Will

SIXTY-SIX

Jake was sitting at the far end of the parking lot watching for Madeline and Kylie. He could see Kylie's car and Jordan's motel room door without any problem. He just wished they would hurry up, so they could get this over with.

His mind was wandering while he was alone. He wondered if he should call Nick, knowing he would have another weapon should things go south. Madeline and Kylie pulled in, interrupting his thought about calling his friend.

The three of them came together at Jordan's door. Kylie knocked, and Jake stood off to the side, not readily visible when Jordan opened the door. Jordan stood back to allow the two women entry as he spurted expletives at Kylie for bringing his mother. He started to shut the door when Jake stopped him.

"What the hell is this all about?" Jordan yelled, trying to push Jake back out. Knowing Jake was the stronger one, he let go of the door and grabbed his gun. "Well, isn't this cozy. Kylie, you want to tell me what's going on?"

Madeline stepped up to face Jordan. "I hired Jake to find you, Jordan. You are out of control, and you need help."

"You what? "Jordan yelled. "You meddling old witch. How could you turn against your own flesh and blood? Now you all have to die."

"Jordan, don't be absurd, this can all work out if you get help. Things can go back the way they were." Kylie was trying to calm her brother down.

"They will never be the same as they were, you stupid bitch. Don't you understand, as long as Father's illegitimate daughter is around and sticking her nose in our business, this will go on forever!"

"What are you hiding there, Jordan, that you don't want Julianne to discover?" Jake asked.

"You shut up!" Jordan yelled. "You should have never gotten involved in all this in the first place."

"Jordan, put the gun down, and we'll all work this out," Madeline coaxed.

"Afraid not, Mother. It's gone too far for that. I'm sorry they had to involve you and Kylie, but I can't afford to leave anyone alive that knows. I will get Julianne later."

Jordan pointed the gun at Jake. Madeline tried one more time to plead with her only son, but it was useless. The determination and fire in his eyes told of the need for him to do this.

Jake reached for his own gun as Jordan fell to the floor. Kylie screamed, and Jake looked stunned as he saw Madeline standing there with a gun in her hand. She was in shock over what she had just done.

Jake reached over and eased the gun from Madeline's hand. She continued to stand there, staring at her son.

"He was going to kill all of us," she said. "I had to do something. He wasn't right. Conrad had said many times over the years that he was the devil himself, and we never did anything about it. We could have prevented all of this if Conrad and I had done something years ago." The tears started to flow.

Kylie took her mother's arm and helped her to the chair in front of the window.

"Mother, it's not your fault. We all knew he was a time bomb and just ignored it." She was sobbing as well.

Jake picked up the phone to call the police. When he hung up, all three of them stepped outside to avoid looking at Jordan's lifeless body lying on the floor.

EPILOGUE

Two years have passed. Kylie and Julianne are sharing ownership of Simms Trading, and the company is thriving. For Julianne the most important thing is that she and Kylie are forming a personal relationship. They are becoming sisters in every sense.

Madeline was never charged for the murder of her son due to the circumstances. "Self Defense," the judge ordered. However, she will be imprisoned within herself for the rest of her life over what she did.

Jake and Julianne were married a year after the incident. They started a family of their own, one that Conrad Simms and Heather Sullivan would be very proud of.

A Stranger in the Will

Author's Notes

My husband and I relocated from Rhode Island to Nevada 18 years ago. We came out to Reno on vacation, we liked it so much we decided to move here. We have never regretted it.

A few years later I started having problems with my legs that required surgery. To keep me occupied during recovery my daughter handed me an iPad and encouraged me to write a book based on a dream I had told her about. Hence, my first book, "Justice for Timmy". I enjoy writing so much my mind began creating....."A Stranger in the Will".

It has been an adventure. I hope you enjoy reading both of them as much as I have enjoyed bringing them to you.

I have an email address below and I look forward to your comments for future writings.

mail@blmarshall.com or on amazon.com on the books review section.

Happy Reading!

CPSIA information can be obtained
at www.ICGtesting.com
Printed in the USA
FSHW021717201218
54579FS